F. E. Wheeler
R. ...

KIDNAPPED

KIDNAPPED

Karl and Debbie Dortzbach

1817

HARPER & ROW, PUBLISHERS

NEW YORK
EVANSTON
SAN FRANCISCO
LONDON

Scripture quotations, unless otherwise noted, are from the *New American Standard Bible* © The Lockman Foundation 1960, 1962, 1963, 1968, 1971. Used by permission.

FIRST EDITION

Designed by Lydia Link

Library of Congress Cataloging in Publication Data

Dortzbach, Karl.
    Kidnapped.
    1. Kidnapping—Ethiopia—Case studies.
2. Dortzbach, Debbie. I. Dortzbach, Debbie, joint
author. II. Title.
HV6604.E82D673   1975   364.1'54'0924 [B]   74–25708
ISBN 0–06–061975–9

75 76 77 78 79 10 9 8 7 6 5 4 3 2 1

Anna Strikwerda and Omer. *S. Andringa*

PREFACE

Missionaries have sometimes been thought of as those people who wear front-pleated pants and skinny ties when everyone else wears bell-bottom pants and wide lapels. Others have regarded missionaries as supersaints impervious to sloppy rainy seasons, detestable food, and mosquito-infested mud huts.

A few people know the truth. Behind the odd clothes and oftentimes plastic smile lie the same problems that face everyone else in the world.

This is a story of fear, loneliness, doubt, and depression—but it is more than just that. The real story unfolds as God's power and peace are evidenced in the midst of great despair.

Without the support of many, it would have been impossible to write this book. Joann Knierim typed manuscript pages far into many nights. Karl's mom completely took over household responsibilities and freed us to devote our time to writing. Bruce Lockerbie offered necessary and sound critical advice. Eleanor Jordan's editing has refined our writing.

And many of you prayed, demonstrated your love in innumerable ways, and encouraged us when writing seemed unbearable. May Jesus Christ be praised.

KARL AND DEBBIE DORTZBACH

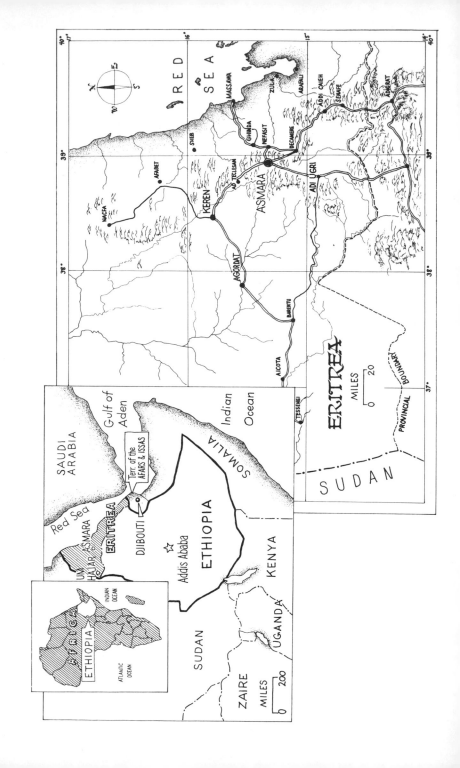

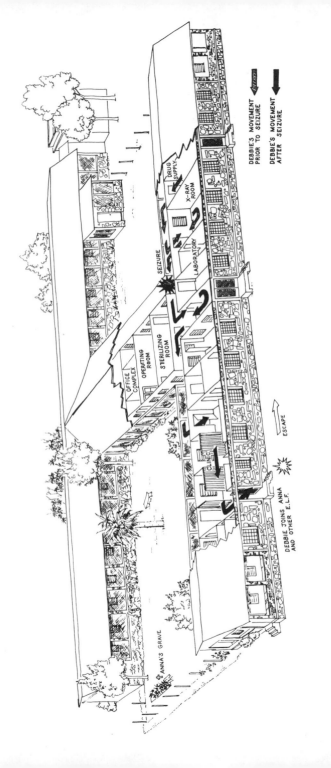

DEBBIE'S MOVEMENT
PRIOR TO SEIZURE

DEBBIE'S MOVEMENT
AFTER SEIZURE

DRUG SUPPLY

X-RAY ROOM

LABORATORY

SEIZURE

OFFICE COMPLEX

OPERATING ROOM

STERILIZING ROOM

CLINIC

ESCAPE

DEBBIE JOINS ANNA
AND OTHER E.L.F.

ANNA'S GRAVE

AUTHORS' NOTE

The names of the Eritreans and of some
missionaries in this story
have been changed.

MAY						
S	M	T	W	T	F	S
				1	2	3	4
5	6	7	8	9	10	11
12	13	14	15	16	17	18
19	20	21	22	23	24	25
26	27	28	29	30	31	

JUNE						
S	M	T	W	T	F	S
						1
2	3	4	5	6	7	8
9	10	11	12	13	14	15
16	17	18	19	20	21	22
23	24	25	26	27	28	29
30						

In this book Karl and Debbie Dortzbach alternate to unfold their respective ordeals, she as a captive, he as negotiator with the kidnappers. A symbol precedes each segment, the open one denoting Debbie's story, the shaded one, Karl's story. —The publisher.

CHAPTER 1

Monday mornings are busy in any African mission hospital. Monday, May 27, was no exception for the Mihireta Yesus Hospital (The Compassion of Jesus Hospital) in Ghinda, in the northern province of Eritrea, Ethiopia. But it seemed unusually busy that day.

I hastily made rounds with our surgeon, Gil Den Hartog. As nursing supervisor, I had to keep on top of things. It would not be easy with sixty beds crowded into wards and jammed into corridors. Ethiopians had thronged to our hospital, seeking Gil's help for polio corrections or abdominal surgery.

Next I made a quick check of all medical patients with Greet Rietkerk, our general practitioner from the Netherlands. Only nine o'clock, I thought, and already the clinic corridors are packed with nearly a hundred people. Muslim mothers swathed in colorful veils nestled bare-bottomed children. Helplessness, pain, and fear furrowed the faces of men topped with spiraling turbans. They came by mule, camel, or foot from uncharted villages distantly settled in the mountains surrounding Ghinda. To show my concern, I wanted to give what I knew of health care and to share what I believed about God. I could give, I could share, but so much of their culture remained a mystery.

Gil rushed by, several wisps of hair visible beneath his operating room cap. He stopped a moment to ask about my leg, since I had been limping around the hospital at a snail's pace. Greet had been watching it over the weekend for a possible developing phlebitis as the pain worsened. Instead of remaining at home that morning, I supported my limping leg with sweaty bandages. The hospital demands forced us all into an unwanted race. No one could afford to be absent. Lives depended upon that pace.

Checking our cholera patients, I found them improved. Lately that ward had kept a constant turnover of patients, all of them arriving on the brink of death at the hospital door. The sallow cheeks, sunken eyes and mouths, and stenching bodies confirmed the grim story. A life lingered at the end of each moment as hours of tense activity were devoted to each patient.

The morning hurried to teatime—a welcomed chance for a bit of rest. Since my first day at work in the hospital I eased into that aspect of the Ethiopian culture. Everyone stopped for tea. Teatime meant mailtime too, but nothing very life-transforming came through the mail that morning. *Time* magazine was still droning on about the Watergate affair, but political controversies seemed oceans away from us.

Resuming my work, I stopped first at the storage room near the clinic for the morning hospital supplies. Delicately balancing an armload of thermometers and medicines, I fumbled with my keys to lock the door. Looking up, I noted that a peculiar quietness had pervaded the packed corridor. Strange, I thought, for people who normally wait in restless impatience. Suddenly I saw the cause of the suspense. Silencing the people was a masked man with pistol drawn. Pushing himself through the standing crowd, he moved toward me.

The Eritrean Liberation Front! Dropping the supplies on a window ledge, I impulsively ran to hide. The darkened doorway of the X-ray room beckoned me. I slipped inside quickly, shut the door, and looked for the key to lock myself in. Still groping, I paused. What a coward, I thought. Surely he just wants something you can get for him, and it will be all over. Go find out what he wants!

My heart pounded through my ears as I jerked the door open

2

and stared straight into the intruder's eyes. Dressed in a dirty-white muslin tunic, his eyes and nose protruding through the sackcloth mask, he pointed a pistol at my abdomen.

Choking over a lump in my throat, I blurted out a question in Tigrinya, the language of the area: "What do you want?" Without waiting to answer, he seized my arm and pulled me past the fearfully gazing crowd to the front entrance. Upon finding the screened door locked, he gestured angrily for me to open it. Frustrated, I tried to tell him I did not have a key to fit that door. He pounded it wildly, then turned and marched me back through the crowded corridor. I looked at the clinic workers quizzically. Why was no one calling the police for help? They only stared back, mouths dropped, motionless like all the others. Then I remembered. The telephone had been out of order all weekend.

Tightening his hand about my arm, the intruder led me through the clinic. A closed examination room gave a desperate hope. "Greet!" I shouted, breaking the stillness. The door remained closed.

The masked man shoved me through an open door, and I gaped at what greeted me outside.

"Don't be afraid, Debbie. The Lord is with us." I marveled at the strength found in Anna's reassuring words. The missionary nurse anesthetist stood dressed in her green operating room gown; a stethescope and mask hung about her neck. With her were four men bracing machine guns and rifles.

At once a swift blow fell on my back. The masked man, walking stick poised threateningly in the air, first yelled at us to run and then cracked the stick sharply over Anna's back. Clutching her hand, we stumbled together down a bank behind the hospital. A trail of armed men directed us toward the northern mountains.

"O Lord, help us!" cried Anna, her voice losing some of its calmness.

"Please help!" I added emphatically. "Oh, He is with us, Anna, at least we're together!"

We tightened our grip. The grass and thornbushes tore at our

3

knees; the noonday sun scorched our skin with a typical 104-degree temperature. Our feet fell unguided in front of us. Feeling Anna's hand on mine reminded me that we never had been that close before. We shared the same profession and similar duties in the hospital, but somehow our lives seldom came together. Anna was fifty-two, but seemed two generations older. She was Dutch, I a Yankee grooved in the American way. She had eight years' experience at our hospital; I was a rookie. But at that moment we were close. Her cold clammy clasp could not have warmed me more. We were together, experiencing much more than mere physical closeness. We were sisters, crying out to God.

"*Keedee! Keedee!*—Go! Go!" the men screamed as they slashed their sticks relentlessly against our backs. High above more men screamed orders from rocky posts.

"Oh, my sandals, I can't keep my sandals on!" Anna yelled as we neared a dry riverbed that led into the mountains. Her single-strapped sandals lay in the brush.

"Try to run on the sand!" I shouted to Anna. A glance at my own sandals told me they would never fit her. Blood-soaked sand ground her blistered feet and slowed her pace. The men tore us apart, their sticks falling like rain. Soon the sand ended; only the biting edge of jagged rocks remained. I looked back to see Anna bent over, putting a sandal, retrieved by a soldier, on her foot.

"*Keedee!*" came the cry from behind as again the stick struck my shoulder.

A muffled gunshot echoed in the valley. I spun around as Anna dropped backward.

"Oh!" I gasped frantically, covering my mouth with my hand. The stinging cut of the stick and the sharp excited demands forbade my returning to Anna. I tripped blindly over the rocky path, stunned by the searing shot. Was Anna in the presence of God?

The men surrounding Anna left excitedly to catch up. One man ran past me with Anna's sandals dangling from the end of his walking stick. I braced my back, expecting an explosive discharge of steel to pierce my flesh. I cried out, "How can I continue, God?

What's happening? I can't go on . . . I can't . . . I can't."

The pace quickened. The path faded as we left the riverbed and approached the steep of a cliff. I surveyed the harsh mountain range ahead. God gave me His answer quietly: "I will lift up my eyes to the mountains; from whence shall my help come? My help comes from the Lord, who made heaven and earth."

"My help comes from the Lord!" I shouted in reaffirmation of Psalm 121. They were verses memorized years earlier when I could hardly have anticipated their impact and strength in the face of instant death. My legs thrust forward. There were mountains to look at instead of the perilous course beneath. A look to the mountains brought peace—not in their beauty, but in the majesty of their Creator, God Himself.

And Karl, I thought. Oh, God, You know I love him. He knows nothing of this. What a shock it will be! We belong together. Make us willing to accept whatever You bring—however long the separation.

From the mountainside came a voice. Another soldier appeared. It took me several seconds to understand his English.

"Don't be afraid," he said. "You see, you are going to help us. You will help our people."

Breathless, I raced on. I already was helping your people, I wanted to shout at him.

We changed direction again, and I searched for some clue to remember the path of our flight. To my left was a hut on the brow of the hill. A useful landmark?

Exhausted, I pointed to my stomach and announced my pregnancy, hoping to gain sympathy. All I received was a puzzled look. Then I begged for water, feeling hopelessly parched. "No," came the curt reply, emphasized by the stick. Just then the English-speaking soldier intervened, halted the beating, and assumed command.

"Here, take this." He handed me a slender walking stick with a crooked end. I dragged it along on the rocks, since I was unaccustomed to using one.

Suddenly another sound cut the air. The choppy interruption grazed over a nearby hill . . . a helicopter! What fast rescue! I thought.

Although I knew that my white uniform surely would be seen easily, I had to suppress an impulse to wave madly. The shove of a frantic soldier sent me sprawling down a ravine into a thornbush. Another stood over me, ordering me to keep low. Gasping for breath, we waited. The copter passed directly overhead and continued in a northerly direction. I expected to hear exchanges of gunfire, for I thought the Ethiopian army to be in pursuit. Soon there was a stirring again.

"Come," said my companion, pulling me up the bank. "It's O.K., you must hurry."

"But I can't . . . I'm so tired . . . If you just let me go at my own pace, I'll keep going. I can't run! I'm pregnant!"

Cries for mercy made no impact. "Look!" I cried, pointing to my arm. Blotches of blood flecked my skin. My face flushed with heat and exhaustion. With a mouth dry as cotton, I croaked, "Please, water!"

Arriving at a stagnant pool, I thrust myself to the ground and guzzled a mouthful before an arm pulled me away. Normally I would have revolted against drinking such water.

As the run continued, my sandals, mere threads holding them together, twisted cruelly as I slipped over boulders. Then my right sandal popped. No shoe! It would mean death! I stopped short. Hanging from a soldier's back pocket was a rag. Pointing to my sandal, I pleaded for it. As he drew it from his pocket, he looked confused and pointed to his own shoe.

"No, no . . . Here." I snatched the cloth from his hand, tied it around my toes and sandal, and continued my run.

The helicopter appeared again, and I realized we were running in a flat clearing. No longer did they attempt to hide me. The copter passed quickly, leaving only the chatter of men and the scramble of sandaled feet.

"How much farther?" I asked wearily.

"Not far . . . about half an hour . . . you'll see."

On the verge of collapse, I begged to rest. Instead, the soldier pulled me up on his back and carried me. Thankful, I slumped my arms over his shoulders; my sandals barely clung to my toes. He lowered me after several minutes.

"Water!" I cried again, spotting a tiny brook.

We stopped, and stooping beside me, the English-speaking soldier filled his cupped hands with water and motioned for me to drink. Three or four times he brought water to my mouth.

"You really are thirsty," he remarked.

"Yeah," I gasped, for I had unwisely swallowed the water so quickly that I felt like belching.

Blood trickled down my leg, and I impulsively splashed water on it.

"No!" shouted the soldier. "That water has some bacteria."

Strange he should warn me against it now, I thought. I just drank it!

"Come on . . . let's go." A hand yanked me up.

The path led down into a small valley. A young boy herding camels scurried to clear the path. I looked at him longingly.

"Can I go by camel?" I begged. I yearned to end the grueling run.

"No," the soldier answered forthrightly, and pushed forward. I cast a lingering look of desperation and hoped the boy somehow would communicate the unspoken message to my mission.

The ascent began again; the chatter of the men heightened in volume. I glanced about, and perhaps twenty more faces peered at me. As the path gave way to the brow of the hill, the men fled. At last I fell prostrate, frozen on the incline.

Looking up, stern eyes gazed at me. A slender muscular frame weighted with an ammunition belt and a machine gun loomed over me. A clean uniform and beard distinguished him from the others.

This is it, I thought. I'll be shot.

"Mihireta Yesus Hospital?" were his only words.

"Yes."

"Your name, American?" He scribbled several notes on a pad as I answered.

"Come," he said, and he led me to the hilltop. Nothing familiar was visible as I scanned the distant mountain haze. Steel rifle muzzles glinted in the glaring sun as my eyes fell on an armed guard.

Turning to the bearded man, I continued, "Yes, I'm a nurse from Ghinda, and I'm pregnant!" Indifference stared at me; the relaxed, unhurried atmosphere told me I stood on their turf.

One of the men pointed to an object a few hundred yards away. The helicopter! My mouth dropped at the sight of a white man standing beside it.

"I'm Debbie," I offered upon reaching him.

"Grant," he announced, smiling. The color of his skin, his freshly laundered appearance, his strong build, stood in contrast to the others.

It's not going to be so bad, I thought. He looks healthy and well . . . he must be one of the men captured several months ago from the Tenneco Oil Company. No word has been heard from them since.

Grant opened the door and ushered me gently into the left side of the transparent bubble. I settled in, flopping my head against the seat. Weary, I closed my eyes and breathed a prayer, "God, I'm alive! Please keep me going."

My thoughts were interrupted as a brown hand reached inside the helicopter window and patted my abdomen.

"Little one here?" he asked in a distinctively softened tone.

"Yes," I sighed, staggered by his tenderness as I looked into his eyes.

"I can only take two others plus myself at the very most," Grant announced to a distinguished-looking figure who carried no gun, wore a fatigue cap, and had the air of an officer. Grant's warning set off a discussion with the bearded leader I had met earlier. Then Grant turned to me.

"How did you get here?" he asked in an academic tone.

"By force."

"Yeah?" he exploded.

All at once the two E.L.F. leaders sandwiched themselves into the copter next to me, the machine gun pointed carelessly at my face.

"We're going to crash," Grant muttered to himself as he pulled back on the throttle. "Sure hope we can take off . . . with four of us."

"Four and a half," I quipped with a nervous laugh.

The blades spun quickly, gaining momentum. The engine deafened conversation. Then slowly the mighty bird lifted off. I looked at my wristwatch—it had been two hours since I left Ghinda.

In the eerie expansiveness the bird crossed the plateau shallowly. With the band of men fading in the background, the men next to me simultaneously pointed north, and the bird followed in the same direction . . . away from Ghinda.

After flying over several small peaks, I breathed easier when the mountains melted into a barren flat desert. Directed ever northward by the waving arms of the leaders, the great bird came to a small irrigated stretch of land, nosed down, and landed. Several loincloth-girded Eritreans hurried to deliver goods: two nylon sleeping bags, a plastic bag of canned items, a box of cookies, and a packaged wooden crate.

"Hey, we can't take on all this," Grant announced defiantly. "We'll crash for sure—we're already overloaded."

Mumbling to themselves, the men rationed out the heavy items. The two sleeping bags along with the plastic bag of canned goods landed on my lap. The wooden crate and box of cookies remained on the ground.

"Hmmm. Looks like we're going to spend the night," Grant said, trying to appear lighthearted.

With another sigh from Grant, and a constant prayer on my lips, he again braved an attempt and carefully the copter was lifted from the ground.

The stark monotony below was relieved occasionally by small

Left: At the heart of Ghinda stands the mosque. Its minaret is seen here, towering over nearby houses and shops. The upside-down cup on a stick in the foreground marks a beer house.

Below: Ghinda nestles in the middle of barren Eritrean mountains. In the foreground at the far right is part of the hospital compound.

clusters of straw-mat huts. The precariously scattered villages seemed to be basking insignificantly in the vast desert land. I wondered if some of our patients had come from there.

The helicopter hugged the escarpment. Ranges of peaks stretched to the left, boundless wastelands to the right. Then pointing westward, the whirling craft was directed into the crests.

"Here goes," Grant announced nervously. "We'll have to circle to gain altitude for this one."

The desert withered into the horizon. Every mountain looked the same.

Desolation swept over me.

"Hello?" rang out Art Steltzer's usually cheerful voice. He was the only ordained minister in our Ghinda mission and each Monday he taught a Bible class in Asmara, the provincial capital of Eritrea. "Gil?" Obviously Gil Den Hartog was on the telephone from his home in Ghinda. I wondered what the doctor wanted. If I did not get another shopping errand, I planned to research a paper I was writing for Westminster Theological Seminary in Philadelphia, about our mission. Eleven short months in Ethiopia seemed inadequate to test my seminary studies and theories in the crucible of life.

"They what?" The urgency in Art's voice jarred my thoughts. His voice then became strained but quiet. "Anna and Debbie? What should we do?" A knot grew in my stomach, and I sat in suspense while Art finished his conversation. Several of us were eating lunch in an Asmara apartment rented by our mission. Hanging up, Art quickly swung back into the dining room where we sat. He stood for a few moments before he spoke. His large six-feet-two-inches 225-pound frame tightened. His square face was drawn and was more the color of his graying hair than its usual pink. His mouth hung in disbelief, while his eyes pierced me with agony. I

11

felt it coming. Whatever it was, it was for me.

"Steel yourself," he finally erupted. "Your wife has been taken. The hospital was raided, and Debbie and Anna are taken captive."

I sat stunned. When Art's words soaked in, it was immediately clear that the Eritrean Liberation Front, a leftist movement that had fought since 1962 to gain complete independence for the northern province of Eritrea, had raided the hospital. Two years earlier the same group had taken medicines and money in a midnight raid. At that time our mission threatened to close should such acts be repeated.

The possibility of a kidnapping had never occurred to me. Anna and Debbie . . . what did they take Debbie for? A thousand questions flooded my mind. My strength poured out of me as fast as they came. Was she alive? Where was she? Why take two? When would they be back? Did they say what they wanted? Where did they go? What were we to do? Finally I asked the obvious: "What happened?"

"Gil didn't say much over the phone," Art replied. "Just that a band of armed men had entered the hospital at twelve o'clock through the clinic and forced Anna and Debbie to go with them, and then forced them to run down toward the east."

His answer burned. Debbie's legs had been painful and swollen when I left her in the morning. Pregnancy nausea upset her nearly every day. Running was impossible. How was she? Did they take her easily? How long would it be? When would I see her again? Would I see her again?

"Wh-wh-whwh . . ." I could not get out the question. Finally I collected myself. "Wh-wh-whaaaat do-ooo we do now?" I stuttered. I never stuttered.

"Gil said we should first contact the consulate, and then go immediately back to Ghinda." Art's voice seemed unusually calm.

It was 1:05. We had begun to eat only ten minutes before. Jim Miner, the hospital maintenance man who had come shopping with us to Asmara, was due at the apartment any minute, so we went back to finishing a few more bites. My mind, however, was not on food. What will we do? I thought again. In fact, what *can* we do? Words tumbled into my head. "I will bless the Lord at all times. . . ." I quickly argued, Not now, Lord. How can I give thanks now? My mind drifted to Debbie, and I could hear her singing the rest of that verse from Psalm 34: "His praise shall continually be in my mouth." We had often sung those lines together. The words rang in my ears . . . continually . . . at all times . . . continually . . . I will bless—Oh, God! Leave me alone! Debbie is gone! My wife, my love—why, God? Why did You do it? My mind went no further; shock shut my mouth.

Jim came and immediately went with Art and me to the consulate. On the way more questions pried into my mind. What did we really know? Nothing. Perhaps Debbie and Anna were back at the hospital. Perhaps no one was even hurt, no money lost—just a lot of shaken-up people.

When we arrived at the consulate, no one was guarding the gate. We rang the gate bell. No answer.

"What's wrong now?" I asked. "Where are they?"

Art, clucking his tongue, summed it up with his usual after-the-fact observation: "I wondered if they would be here, it's Memorial Day."

Of course! Memorial Day is always on the 27th of May! I was furious. Why couldn't Americans leave their holidays alone and have them on the right day, like everyone else in the world? As we stood gaping, a maid appeared to empty the trash. With difficulty we convinced her to bring someone from the house. Moments later Mrs. Perry, the wife of the assistant consul, emerged.

"Is Mr. Perry available?" Jim queried.

"No, he is gone for the day," she replied.

"Is there anyone else from the consulate here today?" Jim pushed harder for an answer.

"Well, yes, what is your difficulty?"

"We are from the Presbyterian mission in Ghinda, and we just received a call from the hospital that two of our nurses have been kidnapped." Jim reviewed the events quickly.

"Oh, God!" Mrs. Perry gasped. She was immediately concerned, unusually concerned, I felt. Her gasp shook my thoughts again. I too had cried out to God, but I wondered if she realized right then to whom she had called.

She ushered us graciously into the front room, pumping us with questions as we walked.

"I'll go get Al . . . he's the only one here . . . you see, my husband is in Massawa; he should be back by now . . ." and her voice trailed off as she quickly disappeared.

(I later learned that Mr. Perry had been having lunch at an Italian restaurant a half mile from our hospital at the very time the E.L.F. made their raid. Mrs. Perry had good reason to be concerned: if the E.L.F. were planning anything big, the American assistant consul would make a nice catch.)

In a few minutes she returned. I wanted to tell her that God had promised strength to overcome fear. I wanted to tell her about faith in Christ—faith that was a demonstrated confidence in the never-failing power of God. But how could I describe what I did not have then? While I was trying to drum up the strength to help Mrs. Perry, Al came in.

Al was in charge of consulate communications; in the weeks to follow he would have a few messages to send. We went over the slim details known about the kidnapping.

On the telephone Gil had reported to Art that the band headed east. That had to be wrong. No road ran north of the hospital. Neither village nor army existed there, only one rugged hill after another. The rocky, barren mountains had provided refuge and security for the E.L.F., and the brutal hiding place stretched for mile after mile. Their flight had to be northward.

After reviewing all the information we had and making all the guesses possible, we could only return to Ghinda. I rode with Jim in our Volkswagen bus, while Art went to the apartment to get his wife and to cancel his afternoon Bible school classes. Jim knew the road to Ghinda well—each tortuous curve. Normally it took ninety minutes to wind down the corkscrew road to Ghinda twenty-seven miles and 5,000 feet in elevation away. The trip back that day took only fifty minutes, yet seemed an eternity.

I was still haunted by what I might find at the end of the road. Everything was unknown. A picture of Debbie flashed into my mind . . .

The freshman initiation picnic at Wheaton College had introduced me to a social life that my one date in high school poorly equipped me to face. When I met Debbie, I marveled that anyone as attractive and popular as she would actually desire medical missions. Unable to win a date from her, I interested myself in a Sunday school class for retarded children—where, of course, she just happened to be working. In our weekly meetings I learned that her family of nine children included three sets of twins. Her own twin brother was afflicted with cerebral palsy. Like me, she had grown up a preacher's kid, she in New Jersey and Canada, I in Colorado. Unlike me, she shared no interest in developing our relationship beyond being simply coworkers.

Teaching handicapped children about Jesus' love had forged a link between us. Mutual respect deepened into admiration; admiration opened into love. Debbie transferred to Columbia University Department of Nursing and I to Georgia State University for a Special Education degree. That separation refined our love. The relationship grew to be triangular, not linear: The Lord was with her and He was with me. In seeking first to love Him and know His love, our lives were knit together.

Before marriage we had attended an Inter-Varsity Christian Fellowship student missions conference in Urbana, Illinois. As we confronted the need for nurses and teachers and the opportunity for short-term mission work, a seed thought germinated in our minds. Three years later when I wanted a break from the academic air, we investigated ways of learning the art of ministering to the needs of others. After two years in Philadelphia, we boarded a plane for Ethiopia, where we would join the mission of the Orthodox Presbyterian Church.

Stepping off the plane had opened a new world for us. Our

third-floor apartment in Philadelphia remained behind. Debbie's public health nursing in the city's ghettos formed a foundation for her new nursing tasks. My seminary academics contrasted with preaching, teaching, and maintenance work. We knew little about Ethiopia, only that it was traditionally the world's oldest Christian empire. Our mission hospital served a predominantly Muslim area of Ethiopia. We had a message to proclaim in word and in deed.

My thoughts continued to race as Jim and I turned the corner onto the bridge that led into Ghinda. I recalled the sermon I had preached the day before. "Are you lonely?", I had begun. Jesus answered, "In the world you have tribulation, but take courage, I have overcome the world." Funny, I thought, that I should have preached that yesterday. I wonder what God is teaching me.

Honking and twisting through the donkeys and goats on the road brought my attention to Ghinda. Rows of whitewashed mud-and-stick houses sped by. At the far edge of town the hospital driveway turned away from the road. People lined the dusty dirt path. Jim eased down the speed, and the yard in front of the hospital came into view. It was jammed with people. Soldiers dotted the area. No one moved and everything seemed strangely still, almost deathly quiet. Swinging up to Jim's house across from the hospital, we saw the other missionaries. As we pulled up to a stop, I broke the silence.

"This is quite a welcoming committee—who's coming?" I tried to be lighthearted. Gil reached me first, his eyes narrowing as he spoke.

"Do you know what's happened?" His voice quivered. In the hospital he would boom out if his medical orders were not followed, and in times of difficulty his voice would be soft and firm. "Anna's dead," he said simply.

Dead? How could that be? She was with Debbie. Then I vocalized the thought that had gone through my mind a few times already. It came softly.

"What about Debbie?"

"We don't know; the army is still down in the valley. So far they have found Anna and sent word for a stretcher. Her body was carried in a half hour ago." Hanging his head, he backed off.

For a few minutes I sat on the house step. I did not know what to think or to say. Everything had happened so quickly. Only that morning I had seen Anna going into the hospital. That same day she was dead . . . and Debbie? I could not face life without her.

"Uncle Karl, are you sad?" Omer's voice broke into my thoughts.

Omer was an orphan that Anna had cared for. His first mother and father were killed in an army raid on their desert village. His brother, the only other survivor, carried him barely alive to the hospital. Anna mothered him and nursed him back to health as her own son.

I looked into Omer's eyes, which were brimming with tears. What could I say? My years of schooling offered no word of comfort. My years of preaching and teaching brought no simple thought of hope or answer for him. Then I heard another voice.

"He's happy *and* sad," said Ruthie. Jim and Beverly Miner's only daughter of seven years, often precocious, set my mind spinning. Her words fit my thoughts exactly, but why I could not quite say. She continued, "Uncle Karl is happy because Miss Anna is with Jesus, and he is sad because he misses your mother, and he doesn't know where Aunt Debbie is."

Exactly . . . that was it exactly. Anna was with the God she had served, and I knew nothing about Debbie.

Our return to Ghinda was a pounding shock. Anna's life had been snuffed out, leaving only a corpse and a tear-smeared orphan. Debbie's flight from the hospital left only empty footprints trailing into the unknown. The army still searched in the valley. Debbie's body undoubtedly would be found any minute. Anna's senseless shooting seemed to seal Debbie's fate too. What would I do without her? It was too short a time that we had been one—surely God would not end it so soon? There were too many things to learn with her, and we were only beginning.

Jim called me off the house step into the living room. Sullen silence engulfed the room as each of the missionaries pondered the events and unanswered questions.

Jim spoke first. "Let's go ahead and pray while we wait for Art." Art had not yet returned from Asmara with his wife.

"Before we do," I interrupted, "I'd like to read a few verses from Romans 11:33–36." I wanted to express a lesson I was learning: that the hardness of the times had hope. I began slowly.

" 'O the depth of the riches both of the wisdom and knowledge of God! How unsearchable are His judgements and unfathomable His ways! For who has known the mind of the Lord?' "

I gulped. Why had God planned for Anna's death, and Debbie's departure, at that particular time?

" '. . . or who became His counselor?' "

My face flushed; I wanted to tell the Lord what to do; it seemed He had it all wrong.

" '. . . or who has first given to Him that it might be paid back to Him again?' "

My voice broke. What could I bargain with God about? All I had were bitterness, pride, and crushed self-confidence. I stumbled over the last part.

" 'For from Him . . . and through Him . . . and to Him are all things . . . to Him be the glory forever. Amen.' "

I could not hold them back any longer. My nose filled and the tears spilled down my cheeks, wet my beard, splashed onto the Bible and soaked into the pages.

After moments of silence someone prayed, then others, but my mind only followed the words slightly. I had failed. My desire to bring comfort to those in the room ended only in tears. I even lacked the inner strength to read about God's strength. The passage in Romans had stripped me naked. I thought I had some strength and some good ideas, but God said He did not need my counsel or my false strength—He had to do it all. I was crushed. O.K., Lord, I thought, if that's what You want . . . do it all.

When there was a break in the praying, I prayed out loud what I had been thinking. "Oh, Father, You who have made and control all things . . . please bring Debbie back. But Father, bring her release in such a way that no one can say they were responsible for it, just You."

The words caught in my throat. Jesus commanded us to pray that His will would be done. Suppose it were better for her to die?

"Lord, if it isn't Your plan to bring her back," I struggled on, "then somehow . . . give me the strength to accept it . . ."

Sniffles and faltering voices continued the prayer session until everyone had prayed. The stark silence returned.

Then suddenly there was a burst of activity. Suitcases and children were hustled into two cars as the Miners and Den Hartogs prepared to leave. Last-minute plans for closing the hospital operations were exchanged. Sickroom vigils would be kept over patients too weak to be discharged immediately. Records and bills would be put in order. Plans would be discussed with the staff. Since nothing could be left undone, six of us would stay to speed the work. We would all live together in the Miner house. Only those without children would stay. Children! I thought of my child yet unborn. Would I have children?

The rain poured down. The sky darkened all afternoon, and at four o'clock it broke loose. Realizing I was shivering, I grabbed someone's jacket and splashed out into the yard. The rainy season had long passed, but torrential downpours were not uncommon in the afternoon. Rivers of water would race down the driveway and wash out the hospital road. I was soaked, but it made no difference as I stood watching everyone pile into the cars. Marilyn Den Hartog rolled down her window, held out her arm to me, and I bent to give her a last hug good-by. She grappled for appropriate words, but none came.

"God bless you," she sobbed finally.

Normally those words would have seemed trite, the perfunctory words of preachers as they stood at the door after a service. But at that moment their significance overwhelmed me. Neither Marilyn nor I could express our helplessness—a sudden, desolate helplessness. Our inability to help, or even to know what would help, drove us to God's strength, which was all we had. His strength was all she could wish me.

My eyes followed the two cars and families as they turned in front of the hospital and then moved down the long driveway toward the road. Perhaps I would see them again in the States in a few weeks . . . or months. The cars disappeared, and my eyes followed the road back. I noticed the four-apartment complex that we had lived in. It was cold and dark. Then I saw the chapel where I usually spent my day. The door and windows were closed. Emptiness echoed inside. I looked toward the hospital. The masses of people who were there earlier had fled in the rain. A handful remained under the carport huddled together, faces drawn and eyes staring. A few army men were strung out between the carport and the workshop. They stood hunched in khaki slickers to shed the rain; long antennae pointed toward the valley as their radios crackled occasionally. Finally my eyes came to rest upon the workshop. Inside the lights were on, and the open door invited me in. My soggy clothes and the water pouring off my hair and into my collar roused me. I moved toward the shop, knowing full well what was going on there.

Two maintenance workers were making Anna's coffin. They thought of her almost as a mother to whom they would go with their problems, certain of a listening ear which would yield a minimum of advice and a maximum of understanding. In their frustration and confusion they were throwing themselves into the necessary work of burial preparations. They had found a piece of three-quarter-inch plywood, strong and not in need of splicing. But the box seemed huge. I wondered if they forgot that Anna was only five-feet-eight-inches tall.

I hung around the shop for a few minutes, asking how everything was going and offering to help. Fortunately they said everything was all right and suggested I return to the house. In contemplation, I lingered. The coffin was for Anna—would one be needed for Debbie? I trudged to the house alone.

At seven-thirty news broke. The lights of a car pierced the house, deserted by everyone but me. The visitor was unknown to me except by name and reputation. His name was Mohammed, reputedly an important E.L.F. contact. His brother was thought to be a leader of the E.L.F., and he himself a "front" man, one who gave knowledge and cover to the E.L.F. from the village and road. I greeted him as he entered, giving a double-handed handshake and a slight bow in customary respect. Communication was impossible, for he spoke no English. Meanwhile, I sent the driver to find the other missionaries.

He sat down, conspicuously choosing the chair that faced the door and window. His eyes darted back and forth, while his face retained a plastic smile. His uneasiness was understandable. The army guard had stayed at the hospital that night, and some of the men were sitting next door on the workshop porch. His after-dark visit would be highly suspicious. Who would come at such an hour? What could he know?

About five minutes later the other missionaries returned. Mohammed began with the traditional greetings, translated by a hospital worker. He was sorry for what had happened . . . all of Ghinda was sorry . . . they had much sorrow and felt great loss over Anna's death . . . it brought grief to their hearts . . . Mrs. Debbie (as she was called by all the nationals) was cause for much sorrow also . . . she would be safe and taken care of . . .

So it went at first. Finally we got down to business. A helicopter, we were told, had flown over the hospital. It belonged not to the E.L.F. but to the Tenneco Oil Company. The helicopter was going to pick up two of the captured men who were sick. Mohammed also said he was informed that one of two things would happen to Mrs. Debbie: Either she would be flown in the helicopter that evening to Asmara, or she would be flown to a safe place to treat the sick Tenneco men. He again assured us she was safe, would be well taken care of, and that we would see her soon. Then, closing with the same traditional greetings, Mohammed went outside, slipped into the car, and was driven off to the village, leaving us to digest the scanty information.

Debbie treating patients in a clinic for children under five years of age.
Sandie Ten Haken

Karl, speaking through an interpreter, explains the relationship between God and man to three church elders during a dry season Bible school.

I sighed with relief; it was good news. In fact it was exactly what I wanted to hear. Debbie would be back safely in Asmara that night or within the next few days. Then my sigh turned into a groan. The information held too much of what I wanted to hear. Mohammed felt it was his responsibility to comfort me. The best way to do so was, of course, to tell me what I wanted to hear. His words, however, did not necessarily reflect the truth. We were almost back to where we had started, only we had a story that might or might not be true.

As I collapsed into a makeshift bed in the Miner house, the facts loomed ominously over me. Debbie was still gone . . . no definite word of whether she was dead or alive . . . no reason as to why the raid . . . or why Anna's death . . . or what would happen next. Loneliness answered me. When I reached out to find Debbie, the cold floor met my hand. I sought to be pillowed on her soft body, but a hard flat cushion held my head. As I turned over, my mattress told me I was alone. Mohammed's words brought no comfort. I remembered Jesus' words: "I will never leave you nor forsake you." It did not put Debbie in bed next to me, but it was hope and strength.

I slept soundly.

Several tiny nomadic huts came into view as our helicopter struggled over the last hefty climb and then began the descent. People emerged from the straw-clad huts and gathered in a flattened area that resembled a river island. Only a trickle of water cut a path around its perimeter. The pilot was motioned to land on the island. As the big bird dropped, men appeared from behind boulders. Dressed in khaki garb and manning machine guns, they watched us from the top of surrounding hills. Others with rifles wore Muslim turbans . . . E.L.F.? The hills were alive with steel muzzles jutting from the shoulders of uniformed men.

Hovering behind cactus as I stepped from the helicopter were a group of women, squinting to block the blazing sun. Several children clutched their mothers' ground-length skirts and began to cry. I felt like exploding with the same fear they were expressing. Clasping the walking stick, I hobbled along a path toward the huts. My legs felt limp and detached from my body, supported only by strings of flesh.

"*Salaam,*" I cried to the women as I passed them. Their eyes peered intently as they nodded in response. The children, unfolding themselves from their mothers' skirts, pressed for a closer look.

Two men slipped into one of the three huts of the village and returned with a cot for me. The roughly hewn wooden frame was balanced on several rocks in a clearing between two huts. Finding it quite stable, I sprawled out on its net of animal skins.

"Do you want water?" one soldier asked.

"Do you have boiled tea?" I replied. "I can't drink anything unboiled—I'll get sick."

"We will get you some," he answered. His voice sounded almost kind. I welcomed the difference in tone.

Not daring to think about anything, I closed my eyes—but was startled by water dribbling down my nose. The sky had darkened quickly.

"Get up!" cracked a sharp voice behind me. Scrambling out of the hollow cot, I followed the men.

The sky opened and the rain pelted down as we scurried into a teepee-style structure. Stacked rocks formed the walls to waist height. Soggy clouds were visible through the superstructure of logs piled precariously above the rocks. It was obviously a storage hut, since it was the largest in the tiny village and filled with grain sacks. The cot was placed at a spot determined to be driest, and the sleeping bag flung over it. I was motioned to lie down. In the fading light I noticed a white face. Grant, too, had sought shelter.

A sudden thunderclap sent me snuggling into the dry sleeping bag. The soft security caressed me. Escape . . . I thought, shutting

my eyes to the strange men and environment about me. Hide
. . . from the rain and bleakness that surround you. God . . . I just
can't understand it . . . Karl, please find me!

Three years earlier Karl and I had been camping together next
to a lake in Maine. Black skies gushed torrents of rain against our
pup tent; the wind clashed ruthlessly with the forest. Inside we held
each other, basking in a freshly realized love . . .

Water running through my sleeping bag rudely interrupted me.
The water-soaked elastic bandages chilled my clammy legs as I
curled them tighter about me. A soldier bent over me to cover the
sleeping bag with plastic and to hand me a towel. In a far corner
another soldier worked to keep a sputtering fire alive. The acrid
odor of smoldering embers, perspiring bodies, and dirty wet hair
hung heavy.

"Here is your tea," announced a soldier. I sat up, reached for
the edge of the hot glass, and thanked him. So eager was I to
moisten my dry mouth with the tea that I burned my tongue
slurping it down.

Although escape into the solitude of my sleeping bag seemed
desirable, my chilled skin prompted me to seek a place closer to
the fire, and I rolled out.

"Whew, it's drizzly, isn't it?" I said to Grant.

"By the way," the bearded leader chimed in, "you're not to talk
to each other. Tonight we will tell you everything."

Oh, God, I thought, why is this happening . . . what is happening? I'm afraid . . . I'm trapped . . . I'm lost. Where is Karl? What
does he know of this? I need him—we need *You*.

They moved me for the night to live with a Tigre family. An old
adde or mother, her face dusky from smoke and furrowed with
years of diligent labor, squat over a fire, stick in hand, to stir
porridge. As the wide-faced jug lost its delicate balance on the
coals, she shifted its weight, the curved bottom burying deeper into
the dirt pit. At the same time she stuck a finger into the hot mush
and slapped a bit on her tongue. She was haggard and worn and

stripped of any feminine graces, yet her face had a peculiar glow, mysteriously illuminated by the fire. She looked up briefly as I entered.

"Coff-fa-la-qui, adde," I greeted her (asking how she was with the only words I knew of her Tigre language, the language of the nomads which was totally different from Tigrinya). Rising from her squat, she grabbed my hand and squeezed it warmly. She smiled broadly, displaying her rotting teeth, as she returned the greeting gruffly and stooped to kiss my hand. With a chest-racking cough, she directed me to sit on my cot that had just arrived. Then back once again at her vigilant post next to the fire, she continued to prepare her meal, frequently eying me. Thankful for the opportunity to rest, I lifted my legs to the cot and pulled the towel over my shoulders. The grass mats lying over the oval stick frame above me reeked with wet stale hay. Often I had wondered what darkened secrets were hidden inside such huts. Many Tigre women and their children were treated in our clinic, and I had longed for an invitation into their huts to introduce me to their culture.

The rain stopped and the village buzzed with activity again. Through the door flap I saw Grant walk by. He returned shortly and handed me a small yellow metal box.

"First-aid kit," he said, looking at my bandaged legs. "From the helicopter. I thought you might need it. Take whatever you want."

"Oh, thank you," I said, unlatching the clasp and surveying the contents. No medicines—but the adequate supply of various bandages might be useful.

Dusk approached. Balking goats returned from the hillsides. A young bare-breasted girl entered with a goatskin bag of milk, which she began to shake rhythmically end to end, swirling its contents. The hut filled quickly with men, who sat in any available space of dirt to await supper. Taking her stirring stick, the old *adde* emptied the jug skillfully of its thick porridge, filled the crudely-carved wooden bowl nestled in her lap, and topped it with the buttermilk. Then she thumped it on the floor before the men, who dug in with their fingers and ate eagerly.

The young bearded leader turned to me and announced in a whisper, "I told you we would tell you everything, Mrs. Debbie, and so I will now."

"By the way, what should I call you?" I asked, shifting on the cot and inviting him to take a seat.

"Yakob is my name. Now you must answer some questions. You have to answer every question." A detailed interrogation followed.

"Do you know who we are?"

"Yes, you are the Eritrean Liberation Front. In fact, do you know my first day in Eritrea was the day you blew up the bridge on the Ghinda road. We couldn't get to Ghinda right away. Do you remember?"

"Yes, the bridge near Nefasit."

The E.L.F. had been quite successful in that effort to make themselves known. The formidable stone bridge spanning a deep abyss had been destroyed. Although a temporary detour had been made, the repair took more than half a year.

His questioning continued. Biographical information was not so relevant as my nationality or the name and nationality of our hospital director.

"And that other nurse that was with you. What was her name, and what country was she from?"

After I replied, he lowered his voice and asked,

"Now tell me what happened with her—what did you see? Of course, we have our own report, but I want to know what you saw."

Yakob wrote on his pad as I described the events surrounding Anna's shooting. Much of the horror blurred my thinking. I failed to understand any of it, nor did I know who shot her. Was there a chance she might still be alive? Could Gil be operating on her right now? My thoughts were answered . . .

"We are sorry for her death and the trouble we have caused you," Yakob interjected. "You see, it is a mistake that we have you."

A *mistake*? . . . A mistake that Anna is dead? . . . How cruel a rationalization . . . What despicable words . . . Streams of attacks bombarded my mind.

"We wanted your hospital director—ah—what's his name again?"

"Den Hartog."

"Yes, him"—and with careful articulation he continued—"for the purpose of getting medicines. Our plan was to take him out into the hills and hold him for a ransom of medicines—just the medicines you had on hand at the hospital, nothing else. Then he would have been released—immediately, even after only three hours. That was our plan."

"You only want medicines?"

"That's all."

"I'm sure our mission will give you anything you want. You didn't have to do all this." Becoming bolder, I added, "We were beaten—I can show you my bruises, and you know I'm pregnant." I did not mention Anna's death again in fear that the accusation would incur anger and perhaps more.

"Yes, I know you're pregnant—but never mind. It's all up to your hospital. As soon as we get the medicines, we'll let you go. You will go by helicopter back to Asmara. It will be only a couple of days."

Days? Fears of what would follow flashed into my mind.

"But all those men," I said. "They all have guns. Can I even go outside to the bathroom?"

Yakob spread out his arms toward the open spaces beyond the huts. "As you can see," he said, "we don't exactly have a W.C. But help yourself. No one will shoot."

"And the hyenas—the goats here will attract them," I went on, remembering clearly a night in Ghinda when the car lights had flashed at a pack of hyenas that sat with their marbled eyes and matted hair, snarling by the roadside. Their barks ripped regularly through the still night air. The endless police sirens outside my dormitory window in New York City several years earlier would have been a more tolerant sound.

"Don't worry, you are safe. Men are all over these hills, guarding all night. Two by the helicopter, one on that mountain, another one over there," and he pointed in various directions.

With that he left. I lay back on the cot. The satisfied sounds of smacking lips filled the hut as the bare-breasted girl took some hot coals and began another fire. Having ground some coffee beans in a mortar, she funneled them into the nozzle of the clay *jebana* or coffee jug and added water. The red coals glowed as she fanned the fire.

Yakob reentered, carrying a large wooden bowl. "For you," he said. "On top there's some canned luncheon meat, rice, then local bread."

"Oh, *kitcha,*" I said.

"You know *kitcha?*"

"Yes."

"Good, your stay will not be so difficult. Things are familiar to you."

Familiar? When a cactus leaf substituted for toilet paper? When fetid animal skins made up my mattress? When strange soldiers bedded next to me?

Unzipping the sleeping bag, I pushed my stiff legs wearily inside. The manufacturer's tag caught my eye: MADE IN PHILADELPHIA.

Would I see Debbie today? Alive?

At six o'clock Tuesday morning my mind was suddenly alert, reviewing the previous events, and then the day's schedule. Anna's funeral was to be at nine o'clock; the grave had to be dug. Her belongings had to be packed and sent to her family. I had to pack our clothes, for as soon as the nightmare ended we, or I, whichever it was, were going home to Philadelphia.

I heard the front door slam as Art returned from a walk around the compound. Usually, he was up early every morning, doing his exercises.

"Are they working on the grave yet?" I asked. The gravediggers were to have come early, because the rain had made digging impossible the day before.

"Since five this morning," Art replied. "They've changed the site, though. Now we'll bury Anna in the courtyard by the hospital. The hospital workers wanted to be able to see the grave, so they would always remember."

"Who's going to conduct the funeral?" Greet asked upon overhearing the news.

"Shall I do it . . . or did you want to?" Art offered without my having to answer Greet's question.

I gladly deferred. I had never preached at a funeral. But if there were going to be a second one, I definitely wanted to do it. Were

I to preach, it would be a strong evidence of God's strength. Would my first funeral be Debbie's?

I moved almost unconsciously to the workshop to check on the coffin. It was nearly finished. The flat black paint still glistened in spots where it was not yet dry. A simple wooden cross graced the top of the long-tapered box.

Then I wandered out to the gravesite. The gravediggers were three feet deep and were leveling off the bottom. A village official was there to oversee the digging. It seemed to me that the grave was too shallow. Consequently, after a few minutes of conversation, I convinced them to dig a full six feet deep. The diggers continued with greater speed. Already the appointed hour for the funeral had been postponed. Another man in town had died and the shumes, or village elders, requested that we have our service later in order for them to attend.

As the hole deepened, I stood at the end of the grave and looked into it. The walls were straight and long. The huge hole gaped in stark reality. Dirt and rocks thrown out of it mounded incredibly high. I was looking into the grim end of life. Everyone would eventually end up in a gravesite at least similar to that one. Anna had chosen to go to Ethiopia as a missionary, but she had not chosen that gravesite. She had no say as to its depth or as to the stone to be placed over it. No matter how we might call out, Anna would never answer. She was dead.

I looked at the pile next to me. That might well be the place of Debbie's grave the next day. She, too, would no longer make choices. She had traveled to Ethiopia with me to tell about life, not death. The irony of it all hit me as I thought to myself: Anna, your body is now dead, and you can do nothing to make it alive, but once your spirit was dead and then God made it alive.

Saddened by her physical death, I was yet heartened that Anna had come to trust in the resurrected Son of God. Anna's death had sounded our message—her message—that spiritually dead people are made alive through trust in Christ. For Anna, physical death had lost its dread.

Villagers gathered around the hospital, wailing as they came. The customary long-drawn-out moaning drilled into my bones. I battled to shut it out of my mind. By eleven o'clock villagers packed the grounds. Peasants stood with shumes, Muslims with Ethiopian Orthodox Christians. Many men from the army, navy, and police crowded together with women and children. Businessmen gathered with school children.

Art and I stood at the head of the grave while the hospital workers filed out slowly, singing and escorting Anna's body. I was thankful that someone else had laid her in the coffin, and that I had not had to view her stiff corpse.

Again I stared past my feet into the grave. Its depth could swallow more than a single body. My thoughts stopped as the coffin came alongside the grave and was set down. My gaze shifted to Art as I anticipated his opening remarks. Instead of beginning right away, he stared at a large group of men who were walking toward us.

They had come from Ghinda, and the clean white turban on each man's head marked them as Muslims. Their solemn air and conspicuous arrival indicated they were the village shumes. Without pausing on the near-distant hill or stopping at the back of the crowd, they marched soberly to the front and formed a line immediately at our side. Those who were bitterly opposed to the preaching about Jesus had come to pay their respects to Anna, an ambassador of the Jesus they spurned.

" 'I am the resurrection and the Life; he who believes in Me shall live even if he dies, and everyone who lives and believes in Me shall never die.' " Art read Jesus' words as he began the service. He spoke and read briefly about the meaning of life and death. He said in effect: Those who trusted that Jesus died to pay the penalty for their sins would have spiritual life forever, even when their bodies were dead and decayed. Anna was dead physically and alive spiritually; she had served a crucified and risen Jesus. Her grave would go on to proclaim that Jesus had paid the debt for her sins. Anna had been ransomed; she was free.

Finally, we moved to lower the coffin. As we swung it into the grave, the long ropes attached to the coffin strained under the load. It sank slowly into the depths of the earth. We dropped the ropes and I stepped back to watch. The long black box seemed hundreds of feet below. The sun was strong overhead, but the moment seemed cold. A life had been snuffed out and a body was all that remained.

Whoomp!

The heavy thump followed the first crashing shovelful of dirt on top of the coffin.

Whoomp! Whoomp!

Each man took turns to move the mountain of dirt. The mouth of the grave swallowed up its contents. The army, navy, and police all brought large floral wreaths and laid them on top.

My mind hung on to the last sight of the coffin as it had disappeared into the ground. It seemed as though death did sting and the grave was final. I was lost in thoughts of life and death as the many people drifted away. I then saw Omer standing near the grave, eying the flowers on the mound of fresh earth. The sound of weeping filled the air, but he remained still.

"Aren't you sad about your mother?" a village woman asked him.

"Yes, but you shouldn't cry," he replied, "because today is my mother's festival. She's with Jesus now."

I thought back to Jesus' words: "Everyone who lives and believes in me shall never die."

The hut was still dark. I strained to see a figure hunched over a pit of coals and nurturing quiet embers with gentle blows. My eyes grew accustomed to the darkness and searched the hut. Curled into a corner was the young girl who had made the buttermilk. Slumped on the floor were three or four men. Then, with arms

A member of the small mission-established church in Ghinda.

outstretched and cavernous yawns, the men sat up. Quickly, the old *adde* put the *jebana* over the red hot coals for coffee. In another pit the men began to roast kernels of corn. I settled back into the sleeping bag, not anxious to meet the first morning of my captivity.

I'm not dreaming, I thought as I blinked at the old *adde*. Only yesterday morning Karl and I had been together and had pulled ourselves away from a comfortable embrace in bed to prepare for the greater demands of the day. As usual, Karl had made breakfast as I puttered around, dressing. After shoving in the last mouthful of pancake, he had gathered a few books and the hurriedly written shopping list and ran out the door to meet the honking car in the driveway. I had not been given a good-by kiss, I remembered. It always was a "must" in our marriage; whenever I would forget,

Karl called me back from the beaten hospital path with a puppy-dog whine, "You forgot to give me a kiss!" Little things mattered in our relationship.

One of the men handed me a glass of coffee and a handful of roasted corn. I ate breakfast gratefully. Then groaning with stiffness and the swelling pain of multiple bruises, I groped for the walking stick and climbed awkwardly off the cot. The dense smoke from the two fires drove me outside in search of fresh air. Then I limped around the huts, wondering how to occupy my day.

The camp stirred; there had been a change of guards. On the distant hills I could see figures winding through the cactus forest as they returned to camp, rifles over shoulders. Not far away stood the helicopter, blades motionless. I was anxious to see them spin, spinning me back to Ghinda.

I lolled over to a large rock, discouraged. As I sat down my attention was captured by a small hard-shelled insect at my feet. It climbed slowly over pebbles bigger than itself, and made its way around my foot. I pushed a small twig in front of the insect to watch it climb over. But upon reaching the stick, it stopped immediately and barricaded itself inside the hard shell. Immobile, its body had become a fortress.

I wanted that same kind of protection. I felt vulnerable, not only to being at the mercy of the men who held me, but also to depression and discouragement. I wanted to retreat, to roll my life into a ball and forget the world I was in. But I could not. I was a prisoner.

I watched the insect put out its legs and continue its journey. I felt God wanted me to learn His concern for the world He created. His design for the self-preservation of all living things was evidenced in all creatures. His design for my life was that I be preserved in Him and protected by Him.

As I continued to watch the insect Yakob appeared from the storage hut and walked toward me.

"Now we will write a letter," he said in a half-whisper.

Taking me into the *adde*'s hut, Yakob pulled from his knapsack carbon paper and a pad with Arabic printing on the letterhead. Upon handing me the pad and a pen, he instructed:

"Address it to your mission and the American consulate. Tell them you are well, and that you will be released as soon as a supply of medicines are paid in exchange. Also, they must contact us within forty-eight hours."

I thought it strange that I should be writing a plea for my own life. But I *was* alive, and I was being allowed to tell the mission. Those were definite reasons to praise God. I sat down and began to write as directed.

". . . I am in an unknown place, held by the E.L.F. . . ."

Unknown place. How true that was! It was unknown to me, but not hidden from God's protection. The insect I had watched a few minutes earlier taught me that.

When I finished the letter, I realized the demands were missing and asked about them. Yakob mysteriously refused to comment. After I signed the letter, I thought of Psalm 91: "He who dwells in the shelter of the Most High, will abide in the shadow of the Almighty. I will say to the Lord, 'My refuge and my fortress, my God in whom I trust!' " I included the reference next to my signature before giving the letter to Yakob.

Satisfied, he started to leave.

"May I write a letter to my husband too?" I pleaded.

After pausing a moment, he again handed me the pad of paper.

I hesitated. What could I write? How could I tell Karl I loved him? My hand quivered; I dropped my head and sobbed. Karl, will I *ever* see you again? I need you. I want to tell you everything you are to me. I want to have you. You are my husband—how is it we are separated?

My thoughts drifted back to university days. As I lay on my dormitory bed, I had often struggled to say in a letter how I loved him. I struggled again. Karl and I had been united for three years only to be torn apart. Being together and developing our love was what we wanted.

"God, You brought us together, and now we are apart. I don't know why, or for how long, but help me to trust You!" I prayed and then wrote:

Dearest Karl,
    The Lord is our strength and our salvation. I am praying God will be glorified—I am praying for you. Please be assured of my constant and growing love . . .
                                        To His praise and in His love,
                                        Deb

I handed the note to Yakob, my cheeks wet with tears.

"Why are you crying? No need to cry," he said ruthlessly.

"Maybe you can't understand," I said, "but I love him."

"It's all up to your mission. As soon as we get the medicines, you will go." With that he left.

I lay back on the cot. The old *adde* watched me curiously through the shadows of the hut. I looked at her withered face and hands. She was about my mother's age although she looked older than my grandmother. Like the women in Ghinda she probably had borne children every year of her marriage, with many of them dying of malnutrition. Only those made of steel, like herself, could survive. She was in her last years, and her steel was melting. I wondered if she had ever known love.

Leaving the old *adde* a few hours later, I went to the storage hut for lunch. Grant sat puffing on a cigarette, while several men hovered near the fire to prepare our "banquet." He joined me when a blackened wooden bowl filled with rice, burned *kitcha,* and canned luncheon meat was carefully laid on a rock before us.

"Guess we don't worry about manners here," Grant said, plunging four fingers reluctantly into the bowl.

"Nope. Here, try this *kitcha;* it's the local bread made from corn."

"Hmmm. You know all about this stuff, huh?"

"Yeah, from Ghinda." I stopped our conversation with that, not knowing how much was too much.

After several bites from the bowl, Grant paused and lit up another cigarette. "I'm not hungry. I need to lose weight," he said. I forced myself to continue, choking down the dry bread. I've got to keep up my strength for the baby, I reflected, wondering how the fetus was tolerating it all. Placing my hand on my abdomen, I tried to communicate with the tiny bundle of life. Nothing seemed abnormal, but I could not be certain. Since my forced march the day before, I kept close watch for possible bloody evidence of trauma to the fetus. I marveled too that my nausea had stopped. Thank You, Lord, I thought. You knew I couldn't cope with that now!

The fire sputtered. Looking to the logs overhead, I saw water dripping through the cracks. It was raining again. The men hustled me back to the *adde's* hut as the rain pelted unmercifully. Grant followed and the hut was soon crowded with soldiers and villagers seeking shelter. Trickles, then streams of water etched a path inside the straw-mat siding. The sky thundered angrily and the blast echoed for several seconds. A young child, interrupted from the comfort of his mother's breast, screamed in terror. Older children clutched their mothers' skirts.

Harrowing fears of what would happen to me in those mountains darted through my mind. I tried not to think, but found no peace in escape. How long could I bear the separation from Karl? How long could I survive on rice and bread? And what about the parasites, the malaria, the cholera, the waiting, the uncertainty? What was left for me?

Nothing—there was nothing left in me. I could not manufacture courage. I could not run to Karl for help. I could not run to the blissful world of forgetting and ignoring.

"God, can I come to You?" I prayed. "I have nothing to bring. You won't reject honest feelings shared with You, will You? Comfort me now!"

The rain stopped as quickly as it had started. The mothers and children sauntered back to their own huts. Flakes of charcoal whirled into the old *adde's* face as she blew into the darkened pit to resurrect the smoldering coals. Her pendulant breasts hung over the fire as she peered inside a clay pot. Yakob had given the *adde* a freshly killed goat. The *adde* and her daughter went to work quickly to prepare the meat, a rare dish for so humble a home. Braiding strings of intestines, she threw them into the pot, boiling with water. The fleshy stench sickened me.

When Yakob returned, I tried to stimulate some social conversation. I was curious to know more about the E.L.F.

"What is your position in the E.L.F.?" I asked a bit timidly.

"That's not for you to know."

The hut was silent for a moment, and then Yakob, anxious to talk about his country, continued:

"Do you know about the history of Eritrea? How we have been subjected to colonialization and imperialism for many years?"

"I don't know much," I confessed. "I've read some of the history."

He talked at length about the opportunities the people of Eritrea would have through the E.L.F. He explained the organization of the E.L.F., its councils, leaders, congressional sessions, and goals. The soldiers received education in the field, I was told, in order to teach the villagers.

"We want to be able to give our people everything," Yakob emphasized.

I realized then that the group was larger than I had expected. Because the language, the people, and the culture of Eritrea differed from the rest of Ethiopia, the E.L.F. were not satisfied with the forced harmony characterized by prejudice and misunderstanding.

"But why have you involved us?" I interjected. "We are not interested in political things. We came with only one purpose: to share Christ and His freedom."

"Yes, I know. You come only with your Bible and your hands to help. We don't want to hurt you. You help us. I went to a mission school so I know all about missionaries. But the most important thing to us is our freedom from Ethiopia."

The fire died. Grant yawned. My cot had been brought to the

storage hut and placed along a stone wall. I was afraid of the snakes living in the rocks and asked Yakob to move the cot out to the center of the hut. Strange I should be afraid of snakes, I thought, when propped next to me on a sack of grain is a machine gun.

Sighing lazily and stretching stiffly, the guard near the foot of my cot welcomed a rising sun. The air was chilly. Feeling snug inside my sleeping bag, I was content to ignore the sun. A teen-age soldier brought a glass of warmed goat's milk and set it on the frame of my cot. Thick skim covered the top; the milk had been boiled. Pictures flashed through my mind of goat herders coming to our hospital with pussy ulcers draining from their necks. I was not anxious to contract tuberculosis of the lymph glands from drinking unboiled milk. I held the glass gingerly as I sipped the sharp-flavored milk. Wisps of goat's hair floated on top. It took courage to finish the whole glass.

From the distance came the monotonous sound of voices in unison, repeating the Ethiopian alphabet. The bleats of goats mixed with an infant's wail. Boys threw pebbles while toddlers played with sticks. Smoke curled through dome-shaped huts while women prepared sweet spiced tea. Grant strolled by, puffing listlessly on a cigarette. The forced silence between us ate into me.

In an attempt to save ourselves from complete isolation, he sat down and we talked hesitantly about families. I spoke proudly about Karl.

"He has a beard," I said. "All the townspeople call him 'Keshie Karl,' meaning pastor or priest. He's really a seminary student. We came over here to get a break from the academic routine."

"You got a break all right!"

"Yeah . . . You have a family?"

"Two kids in Canada. But I don't see them often. In my job I travel a lot. I came to Ethiopia with Tenneco several months ago. Worked in southern Ethiopia in a desert. There security was really tight—had a dozen army men guarding us constantly. Lot of good it did me. Look at me now!" He paused for another drag. "Yakob says I'll go back to Asmara when the helicopter gets more fuel," Grant continued more boldly. "But I'll believe that when I see it. It's stupid we ran out of fuel. I could've carried more, just never expected all this. I was told this trip would take only one hour—then I'd be back in my hotel room. Huh! What's more, that helicopter shouldn't even be flown now. It's long overdue for an engine overhaul."

Our conversation ended abruptly when Yakob appeared.

"Let's go," he commanded. Grant jumped to his feet and headed with him toward the helicopter. Eager to follow, I lurched forward, nearly tripping over several rocks on the path.

"No, not you, Mrs. Debbie. Wait."

The words were bitter. I stood frozen as both of them disappeared over the edge of the plateau. Within minutes the copter was in the sky and flying back in the direction from which we had come. Without me.

I returned to the storage hut. They were gone. Even Grant had left me. I threw myself on the cot, wanting to lash out at the new faces surrounding me in the hut. New faces and soldiers were no longer a surprise, for men routinely came and left the post.

"Mrs. Debbie, never mind. You will help our people." A young soldier was reassuring me with the familiar line. He introduced himself as Berhane. "How are you?" he continued in English.

Berhane could be singled out easily, for he was unusually tall for an Eritrean. He told me he had been with the E.L.F. two years. He apologized that his English had deteriorated from lack of use since he finished the twelfth grade. There in the mountains he spoke only Arabic, the official language of the E.L.F., and Tigre.

Next to Berhane sat a man with a mustache who flashed a toothless grin and called himself Sayeed. He was the only soldier I had seen who wore long trousers instead of shorts. A red bandana was tied around his neck, a short wet stick hung out the corner of his mouth, and a pistol was holstered under his shoulder. I looked him over curiously, for he was a good deal older than the other men.

The conversation ended and the men settled down for a rest, flopping on grain sacks, Grant's empty cot, or a bare spot on the floor. Picking up my walking stick, I trudged out the hut entrance for a change of scenery. I felt freer to move around, although my stiffened body and broken sandal slowed my pace. Sayeed, noticing that my sandals were no longer navigable, called out to me in Tigrinya with Berhane interpreting:

"Mrs. Debbie, give me your sandal. We want to get you another one. What is your size?"

Get me another sandal in the wilderness? I thought we were several days away from any store. Besides, I did not want another sandal; I was not planning to stay that long. I could put up with the inconvenience of my own sandals temporarily.

"Never mind," I replied defiantly. "I don't need another sandal. I only need to go back to Ghinda."

My plea was ignored. The men who went shopping for tea and sugar carried my sandal to match the size.

Later in the afternoon I was lying in the hut, my mind battling boredom, when the sounds of chopping blades cut the stillness and sent excited shivers down my spine. Jumping from my cot, I reached for the first-aid kit and the elastic bandages—my only belongings—and hobbled outside to greet the helicopter. As it landed, I hurried toward the flat riverbed. Surely the men had a response from the mission and would release me. Why else would the helicopter have returned?

"Hold it!" A guard halted me with his rifle. Others ran on to greet the men who were emerging from the helicopter. I waited and watched.

Grant waved and I waved back. I shuffled my feet, marking time in place. To stand still was unbearable. Several boxes were lifted from the helicopter and handed to some of the villagers. Then the door to the big bubble shut Grant, Yakob, and an unidentified man inside. The villagers and guards stepped back as the swirling blades lifted the helicopter and carried it in a westerly direction.

I was left.

My eyes barely focused on the villagers as they mounted the incline toward the huts, boxes balanced on their shoulders. With splashing hotness the tears fell to my cheeks. I did not want to control them. I did not want to stand there frozen. I wanted to muster all the strength I had and run after the helicopter madly; at the same time I wanted to shrink into a ball, motionless on the ground, and forget everything. Hanging my head, I cried out for Karl.

A woman stood next to me, watching. A dirty worn veil covered her head and barely dropped over her shoulders and breasts. Every contour of her slender body was visible through her shabby wrap-around skirt. She nursed a child, straddling his bare bottom over one hip. The child released his lips, peered at me briefly, then anxiously lifted the overstretched breast to his mouth and resumed sucking. I remembered the woman from the afternoon it had poured when she and her children sheltered themselves in the hut.

The mother was young, perhaps younger than myself. I wondered what she thought of me as she stood there. I longed to sit down with her and share everything I felt: my yearning for Karl . . . my loneliness and fear . . . the child that I held within me . . . Would she understand? I needed somebody. With my lower lip quivering, I greeted her. I looked at her eyes. They were wet. She was communicating to me the only way she could. She knew so little about me, yet she cared. I held out my hand awkwardly. Grabbing it, she squeezed her leathery fingers around mine. God knew I needed comfort.

The young woman went to her hut as dusk approached and goats and cattle returned to the village. Herded by young boys, the cows lopped lazily into their fold bordered with cut-down cactus plants. The goats were shoved into small stick-frame shelters. Soon there would be milk for supper. From within the tiny huts flickering flames welcomed family members to their meal.

My cot had been placed again in the old *adde*'s hut, so I entered and settled down to my own meal of the inevitable *kitcha* and canned meat. I watched as the *adde* finished preparing the evening porridge and as the *adde*'s daughter made coffee for the village men. Two fires burning in the poorly ventilated hut left me choking on my supper. I found a vacant spot on the dirt floor and squatted on it, hoping for cleaner air. Although I was not heavily mushroomed in smoke, the odor of unwashed feet and heavily perspiring bodies was no improvement.

As the men slurped the hot coffee, I wondered what they did all day. The women combed the mountainsides in search of wood. They carried water from a half-hour distance away, cared for their children, ground the corn into flour, prepared the porridge, fried the *kitcha*. What was left for the men to do? I could see only that they visited with one another, took long afternoon naps, and drank coffee. I had learned earlier that harvesting had just ended. Undoubtedly, planting and harvesting were hard times. Earlier in the day I had seen a plow resting against the side of a hut. I would have mistaken it for just a stick had not one of the E.L.F. told me what it was.

The stifling room nauseated me. Unable to take it any longer, I convinced the soldiers that my cot should be moved outside. There the huts were silhouetted against a brighter sky lit by the full moon. Forests of cacti could be seen distinctly in the mountains about me. I thought of escape. It was light enough to see my way. But what was the right way?

One month before the Den Hartogs, Karl, and I had sought to take advantage of the full moon. The Red Sea was at low tide, shelling would be good; we decided to spend the weekend at Massawa, the seaport town thirty-five miles from Ghinda. We used every opportunity to snorkel and swim, since we knew that by our next free weekend Massawa would be too hot to enjoy.

I wondered in what direction the Red Sea lay. I thought I had some idea, since I had seen the Muslim men facing toward Mecca while praying, and Mecca was just the other side of the Red Sea from Eritrea. As I gazed at the moon, I could think only of that earlier weekend. It had been so special for Karl and me. Weekends away from the hospital responsibilities were a rare treat, and a trip to Massawa even rarer. We had come back refreshed, just from having been with each other. I longed for that opportunity to recur.

It was on that weekend, too, that I had started a personal study of the book of Second Corinthians and had pondered over several verses. Their paradoxical meaning held little significance then, but I realized all at once that the study had been a preparation for my current experience.

". . . afflicted in every way, but not crushed." I had only to look several feet to see the trouble surrounding me. Little comfort could be derived even when the soldiers attempted to reassure me. But there was the touch of the young woman's hand, the tears in her eyes. God *did* care.

". . . perplexed, but not despairing." Why was the hospital raided when we were so busy helping people? Why was Anna killed so senselessly? How could I survive the mountains and keep my baby? Why should I be so far from Karl when we were meant to be together as one? Perplexing questions, without answers. I kept asking them a hundred times. But perplexity was not devoid of hope. Hope could not be in self. Hope was in Jesus Christ, for the promise was to me that the same power that had raised Him from the dead could also raise me from despair.

". . . persecuted, but not forsaken." All my own resources were sapped. I had no friends to confide in, no satisfying work experience to turn to, no husband's shoulder to cry on. But I was not forsaken. God promised never to leave those whom He loves . . . and He even yet loved me.

The few of us who had remained in Ghinda worked diligently to complete the details necessary for closing the hospital. As soon as possible we would join the others in Asmara. In the afternoon of Anna's funeral I walked toward the apartment that had been our home to begin my part of the work, packing Anna's

Left: Woman spins cotton while waiting for tuberculosis treatment at the hospital clinic. Hair style and lack of head covering indicate she is Ethiopian Orthodox.

Below: A camel, the common form of transportation for nomadic Tigre people, awaits its owner's return from the hospital. Tied to its back is a typical cot with hand-carved legs and simple frame.

personal effects and our own goods. When, and if, Debbie was released, we would leave immediately for the States; our return would be a month prior to our original plans.

Once inside our apartment, I opened the windows that had been closed the day before during the rain. It was stuffy and hot. Dust would soon settle on everything in sight until the next rainy season. Our two-room apartment was helter-skelter. As I looked around the room, wondering where to begin, reminders of Debbie were everywhere. The couch-bed, with the unfinished cushion covers she had been working so hard to make, sat empty beneath the window. In the kitchen, meat molded on the counter where she had left it the day before to thaw. It was for a special lasagne dinner that never was fixed. Several letters she had written lay on the desk, stamped, sealed, and ready to mail. I contemplated adding a post-script to bring them up-to-date before I sent them.

While getting down the suitcases and duffelbag I thought about the day we had packed excitedly for our trip to Ethiopia. Time seemed incredulous! Only a short year earlier I had struggled to push Debbie's dresses into the already rock-hard duffel bag. Packing for a year meant clothing fit for sweltering heat and slimy rain.

How different everything was! I spread out our clothing on the couch. Many of Debbie's dresses had never been worn. They were either too hot for the climate or too short for the culture. Many of our clothes were faded and ragged, having been rubbed together, scrubbed on the washboard, twisted dry, and left to hang in the blistering sun. Some of Debbie's dresses did not fit any more.

I reflected on the promised child that caused the dresses not to fit. In Philadelphia we had never planned to start a family. The unexpected pregnancy required some mental adjustment to the responsibilities of fatherhood. Then gradually early plans and preparations filled us with excited anticipation. What of the present? Was Debbie still being beaten or forced into a grueling run? Would her harsh treatment injure our child? Would it be born maimed or crippled? Would it live at all?

I turned to pack our books, selected the Ethiopian curios I

thought Debbie would want, and then looked at the massive pile of belongings that were laid about: Debbie had not so much as an extra pair of underwear with her—much less a dress—and probably no water to wash in. With no reason to think she would be returning with me to the States, I packed our clothes in separate suitcases. No need to repack should I be facing the flight home by myself . . . Finally cramming the last shirt and skirt into their places, I closed the suitcases and laid all our things to one side, setting Debbie's well-worn guitar on top. We had played it many times to sing about the faithfulness of God, His love, His care, His providence, His mercy, His wisdom. The beaten-up case reminded me that God's hand was still upon us.

The piles of luggage and boxes made everything seem so final. I had hoped that our going to Ghinda would lead us into a life-work. Instead I was turning the corner into uncertainty. How, or what, would I continue? It was to have been the beginning, not the end. We wanted to return to the States exuberant, not defeated, from our year's work. Our marriage relationship had deepened in the last year, but to what avail? Gone was the hope of a child, gone was the love of my wife.

The door clicked shut as I left our apartment and entered Anna's. Art's wife had already begun the dismal task of packing Anna's things, and I offered to help her. Anna's belongings were heaped all over the place: books, papers, pictures, purses, vases, baskets, knitting, paintings, drawing supplies. Some were to be packed, others discarded.

Besides being a nurse, Anna had been a scholar, a writer, and an artist. She had lived such a full and active life that packing became difficult because so many things she had begun were almost finished. She had left them for another day, but that day would never come. She had other things to do now; even as Omer had said the day before, she was with Jesus, she would be praising Him. Painting, writing, and nursing had ended for Anna. I wondered about the things that Debbie and I had planned and whether we would ever do them. So many things remained undiscovered, so much we wanted to do was left undone. Our future seemed to have ended.

With the packing finished, the lids were screwed onto two crates and one large sea trunk, and they were loaded into the mission truck. A few more minutes were spent tidying up the place . . . no one knew when we would be back, if ever.

All remaining missionaries were to leave Ghinda on Wednesday afternoon. They would go to Asmara to await further word regarding the feasibility of reopening the station. The plan troubled me.

Everyone go? I can't go, I kept thinking to myself. Debbie is perhaps somewhere near Ghinda. I can't leave without her; information will come here first. I must be here to receive it.

At lunch on Wednesday I broke the news: I would not be going with everyone else. I would hide in the hospital, keeping enough food supplies for several days. The hospital was in the shape of a large capital H. In the center was the office and operating room complex. It contained a shower, toilet, and windows that viewed both courtyards. It would be a perfect place to stay. Only one or two hospital workers would be told of my presence. Thus if information came about Debbie, I could act on it without arousing the suspicion of the army. The answers were all worked out, and I would not be convinced otherwise. Since everyone understood how I felt, no one pressed very hard.

When the army came to escort the cars to Asmara, I sat securely in my five-by-seven-feet "cell" that once had been an office but felt more like a stewpot. I tried to relax after my mad rush to pack and watched the circulating fan slice through the thick still air. A week before the office had buzzed with activity. Debbie's desk, once piled high, was empty. Chairs, once filled during lively teatimes, stood vacant. Dinner was cold: spaghetti with a touch of tomato sauce and no meat. I thought of Debbie's promised lasagna dinner. When darkness came, I bedded down on the operating room table where once Anna had administered anesthesia to save lives.

I did not wait long for information to trickle in. After only one night a mission envoy came to say that Asmara rather than Ghinda was the place of action. Nearly all missions in Eritrea had closed their stations, and an informant reported Debbie far north of Ghinda near a village called Afabet. Reluctantly, I left Ghinda with the envoy and was driven toward Asmara. The hospital stood empty: no cars, no playing children, no crowding clinic patients . . . only a few leaves blowing in dusty gusts of hot air.

In Asmara, missionaries ran around like headless chickens. Some had scurried to security in Asmara for fear, others had left their hospitals, clinics, and village development plans in protest of terrorist actions. All of us had in common a prayer for Debbie's release; only God's hand, rather than our cunning, toil, or devices, could effect the release. I was to stay at the Sudan Interior Mission (known in Ethiopia as the Society of International Missionaries) along with the Miners and Den Hartogs. The other missionaries— the Stelzers, Greet, and Sandra—stayed at our mission apartment.

After supper I sat down to read God's words and to pray. I needed His strength and encouragement while waiting for some helpful information. My meditation was cut short.

"Art's on the phone, Karl!" Jim had burst jubilantly into my room. "He says that Saleh came from Ghinda on his motor scooter. He followed a letter addressed to the mission. He's still at the apartment."

My heart leaped. It was seven-thirty and the road had closed at six o'clock. It meant that Saleh had come through three road-blocks. Jim and I hurriedly drove to our apartment where we found Saleh hunched in a chair with several coats over him and sipping hot tea. The night and cold mountain air of Asmara's high altitude made his teeth chatter.

I knew Saleh well. His home was Decamere, a small town south-west of Ghinda. His father was a goldsmith, and Saleh had been working at his uncle's flour mill in Ghinda.

He began to tell us all he knew, his dark eyes dancing on a slightly handsome face, his hands gesticulating wildly.

About five o'clock that evening a private truck had been stopped on the road at gunpoint and the driver was given a letter addressed to the mission. The driver later stopped for a drink at a beer house in Ghinda and told the owner what had happened. The owner, interested in helping us and skeptical that the letter would reach us, summoned Saleh to keep track of it. Ducking under the roadblocks, Saleh followed the truck which had special permission to travel at night. Once in the city, he watched the truck enter a large living compound near the brewery.

Scarcely had Saleh finished speaking to us when we pulled him back into the night air, eager to locate the letter. Gil and Jim followed in another car while Saleh directed me toward the house. A high stone wall encircled the corner lot compound, with a large steel gate providing the only entrance. Saleh and I approached the doors while Jim and Gil sat in their car a short distance away, watching. We knocked; no answer. After several knocks and calls the guard finally stirred and opened the gate a crack. Saleh exchanged greetings. No, the master was not home, we were informed, for when his truck had returned, he left with the truck driver.

Our letter undoubtedly had caused the sudden exit of the two men. Not knowing quite what to do next, we drove to the consulate to talk it over.

"Any hope of finding the letter tonight?" Bob Perry, the assistant consul, asked. He emphasized the urgency of finding it, since the letter could be destroyed easily. More than likely the driver and owner would not want to become involved in any E.L.F. activity. As intermediaries they would certainly be implicated.

There was no reason for all of us to continue looking, so Jim and Gil went home. I returned to the car where Saleh had been waiting.

"Think we can find that letter?" I asked.

"I don't know," he answered, "but I know that the man who lives there is important in town and probably we can find him."

Already it was nine-thirty. We sped back to the compound near the brewery, for the later the night became, the less likely were we to find either the man or our letter. At the gate the night breeze chilled my back as I perspired nervously. Although I knew practically nothing about the man who held the first letter that had come about my wife, I felt that for some reason he was keeping it from me. Was he connected to the E.L.F.? Was he just avoiding a position as intermediary? What motivated his sudden departure? To find him would be like trying to isolate a particular fish in the Red Sea.

Again it took several minutes to rouse the guard and exchange greetings. Somehow Saleh managed to befriend anyone whenever he wanted to. He pressed for an answer until the guard gave him two places where the owner usually spent his evenings. One was at a nearby gas station where some friends worked, the other a large club a few blocks away.

We tried the gas station first, but without success. They scarcely knew whom we talked about.

Speeding off in the other direction, we approached the club. I slid to a stop on the rough gravel road. Saleh jumped out and strolled in alone as I eased the car ahead where I could watch through the window and open doors. He talked to a few of the men at the pool table, then disappeared. What seemed like half an hour later—actually only several minutes—Saleh stood at the gate talking with a man who waved his arm in another direction. We had somewhere else to go. I started the engine, getting ready to move.

Our man had not been at the club that evening, but Saleh had more information. In fact, he had several bits of information. The man was known as Haile, he was an important businessman who was seen regularly with two other well-known friends, and almost every night at nine-thirty he could be found at a certain bar downtown.

I glanced at my watch. Ten o'clock—it might be too late for him to be at the bar. We raced through town and parked across the street from an open cafe-bar. Saleh went inside, talked quickly with the bar girl, and returned to ask me in. He wanted me to convince her that it was important for us to leave a note for Haile. The girl, who was expecting Haile shortly, had refused to believe that Saleh really knew him. My white face, however, was proof enough to her that someone important was looking for Haile. I left a brief note and my name, saying I would be back.

We had to move on. With no fresh tracks to follow, all we could do was to try to find a friend of Haile's. Saleh made several inquiries before we could locate the friend's house. Street addresses were meaningless; one needed only the right area, and then asked for the individual by name. We went to a large factory building near our mission apartment. Saleh slipped inside and was gone for twenty minutes. It was customary, of course, that a visitor not just rush in and out. Saleh knew his lines well and certainly he knew how to be sociable. When he came out, he announced that the friend, Dahar, would come with us. Saleh had told him who we were and why we were looking for Haile because he felt that the man could be trusted. He explained that Dahar had been the police chief in his home village of Decamere a few years before. He knew all the places where Haile went and would help us find him. I was skeptical, especially at ten-thirty.

In a few minutes Dahar joined us. He was a short, stocky man who moved in a determined, efficient manner. I gave him all the respectful greetings I could. Our hunt then began in earnest.

We returned to the cafe-bar in town. At least we had not been all wrong in going there before. Still, Haile was not present.

"It's strange," said Dahar as we pulled off. "Almost every night we meet there. I couldn't go tonight . . ." His voice trailed off.

Next we tried The Alayn, a classy American-executive-style hotel. We cruised by the parked cars along the street. Dahar searched them carefully.

"No, it's not here," he said.

"What's not here?" I asked.

"His car—it's a black Mercedes-Benz."

Then he directed us to a house not far away. I did not know whose house it was nor its possible connection with Haile, but Dahar seemed to think he might be there. We stopped at the house and Dahar went to talk to the guard. A minute later he returned to say that Haile was not in the house either and that we should head back to The Alayn. It was eleven o'clock.

At the hotel we searched the parked cars. Then we saw it—a black Mercedes-Benz 280 sedan. None but the wealthiest could afford such a car. We stopped at the hotel entrance and Dahar went inside. In a few minutes he reported back.

"He's not here now, but he has been; he left in another car with a man called 'the Major.' "

I surmised he was called "the Major" to disguise his identity. I knew that he had acted as the intermediary for the Tenneco men captured two months earlier by the E.L.F. Things began to smell suspicious—why would Haile have gone to "the Major"?

Dahar was the only good lead we had, but the trail ended at the black Mercedes-Benz. Eleven-thirty. It was hopeless for the night, and maybe for the next day as well. I wondered what purpose the Lord could have in frustrating me again. I wanted so much to see His powerful hand change the events of the night. I knew that what was futile He could make successful, but still . . .

We drove back to the cafe-bar for another look. Dahar thought Haile might finally be there. If not, then he did not know where to go. But the cafe-bar stood deserted. My heart sank.

"There's one other place," said Dahar almost in passing. "We can try it. I don't think he'll be there, but let's try." He had sensed my disappointment, but his dubiousness was no consolation.

Off we went again until we came to a section of modern Italian-style compounds and houses. We turned up a dark street, drove three blocks to an intersection, and turned down an even smaller street.

"Go slow," Dahar warned, since it was too dark to see easily. We stopped at last in front of a large building dimly lit by a single lightbulb outside. Dahar left the car, walked back three gates, and entered without knocking. Obviously he had been there before. We waited another fifteen minutes. Saleh said that Dahar would find our man, but at midnight I felt it was a lost cause. The entire city had gone to bed and would begin a new day in five hours.

Eventually three men came out of the gate. They stood talking a minute, and then one approached us. I recognized the short figure as Dahar. He came to my window and said that Haile *was* there, but had no letter. I smouldered with hatred. Their lying and withholding hurt me, and I wanted to get even. Dahar sounded too convinced; I knew the letter *had* to be with Haile. If Haile were there, so was the letter. I would get it out of him no matter what!

Courtesy demanded that Haile meet me after the news had been broken by Dahar. I stepped out of the car and walked toward the man who came toward me. He was slender and tall. His six-feet-four-inches towered over me. His face was thin and even in the dim light I could see his wispy mustache and piercing eyes. His handclasp was firm and determined.

"Haile?" I asked. "You have no letter for me?" I tried to be calm.

"No," came the deep, emphatic reply. "My driver only brought me a message that tomorrow I would receive a letter for you."

"Haile, I have been told by people that saw the letter that you have it." I was determined. He was not going to still my efforts.

"I'm sorry. I have no letter," he said, dropping his eyes. Then, turning his face toward the darkness, he continued, "Tomorrow when I receive it, I will tell you."

We left. There was no use pushing further. Obviously he was lying, and Dahar was covering for his lie. I drove Dahar home, thanking him for his time and help. Saleh went to stay with a friend.

Friday morning, May 31, could not come too soon, and even though the frustrations of the night before had left me ragged, I still awoke early. The letter! I had been promised it for that day! The wait was agonizing. About ten o'clock Haile telephoned to direct me to a building near the brewery. Jim accompanied me to the office where Haile sat behind his desk. Without any preliminaries, he handed me not one, but three letters. In spite of my hateful heart, the Lord had answered prayer.

3

Grant returned in the helicopter Thursday, May 30, with Yakob. Sitting down next to me in the hut, he started to talk about his recent jaunt.

"Whew, it was hot in the desert last night! Say, did you know there are girls in the E.L.F.? I saw them—knapsack, grenades, and all!"

Several young soldiers entered the hut and began to question Grant in English about helicopters and flying. I listened to his answers. Since the confines of the hut held little to stimulate one's mind, I eavesdropped on any conversation I could understand. The soldiers listened intently with boyishlike envy as Grant described the mechanics of operating a helicopter. His topographical map of the area intrigued them, and they pored over it as they tried to locate exactly where we were. I too itched to know but felt it was risky to ask.

Yakob entered and motioned for me to come with him. Leading me outside, he announced, "I'm leaving."

"Leaving?" I echoed in response.

"It is time for me to go," he continued. "Many others have already left. I am going down to the plains. Maybe word of your release will come. I will wait there for it. It is all up to your mission." And slinging his machine gun over one shoulder, he strapped his knapsack to his back and walked away.

"When?" I yelled. I wanted to grab his shirt and drag him back. "When can *I* leave? I *can't* stay here!" He did not stop to answer. I cried after him despairingly, "I'll die in these mountains!"

I felt empty. Alone. The only leader I could communicate with was gone. No decisions were made without him. The guards left behind only obeyed; they did not order. Orders by messenger took days. The "few days until you are released by helicopter" would never come.

Overwhelmed by Yakob's sudden departure, I stalked over to where several women had gathered near the storage hut. An assorted pile of woven straw mats and long sticks lay on the ground. I learned I was about to have new neighbors.

I found a rock to sit on and joined the women, which apparently pleased them, for they chattered excitedly. Frequent interruptions from a screaming child that wanted to nurse, or from a toddler scrapping with a playmate or hanging onto the tail of a young goat, failed to bother them. The sun was setting and darkness was closing in, but they continued at a leisurely pace, pulling mats over the hut frame.

The woman whom I had met the day before when the helicopter departed came and sat down next to me. I greeted her, then pointing to myself, I gave her my name.

With a nervous laugh she made a feeble attempt to imitate the sound of my name. I repeated my own name, and then pointing to her, I tried to learn hers. Understanding my gestures, she told me her name was Fatna. That did not surprise me; the firstborn girl of any Muslim home is named Fatna, after Mohammed's important daughter. Fatna's husband Bekeet busied himself with E.L.F. activities. I had seen him several times, although seldom with his wife. He looked about twenty years older than Fatna.

I yearned to talk to Fatna about my family and what we were doing in Ghinda. I knew the word for marriage in Tigrinya, but since I was unable to formulate a sentence, I merely attached a personal pronoun to it. She seemed to get the message, although Tigrinya was not her native language. Then I pointed to my stomach and also to her child, sharing with her that I was pregnant. Her face lit up as she rambled on in Tigre. The other women, engaged in building, glanced at me sympathetically. It seemed strange to them that I, still a bride in their eyes, should be in the wilderness. In their culture I should be stashed away in the shadows of a hut, unseen by the world, until the birth of my first child. The women stopped their work and gathered around me, their curiosity renewed.

Feeling awkward under their scrutiny, I diverted their attention by pointing to the bracelets on Fatna's arm. Pleased at my interest in her, Fatna showed me her other arm, and lifting up her skirt, her ankles. They were decked with colorful beads and thick metal bracelets. She slid her hand up and down my unadorned arm. I pointed to my left hand to show her my engagement and wedding rings. She pulled my hand to her eyes for a closer look. That such small pieces of jewelry could reflect my husband's love for me was apparently unsatisfying to her. She reached to her wrist, slid off one of her bracelets, and handed it to me. Her eyes sparkled as I tried unsuccessfully to force the narrow band over my hand. Fatna too tried and failed. With a giggle she returned it to her own wrist. She then removed a beaded bracelet from near her shoulder, and fitting it over my hand, pushed it up to my elbow. A second woman who was watching the exchange of friendship slipped off one of the heavy metal bracelets from her ankle, and after several attempts, squeezed it around my wrist. Both women held up my arm proudly for all to see.

Their interest next turned to my long, straight hair. Removing the rubberband I used to keep it in place, they combed their fingers through my hair. I pointed admiringly to their own hair. The tight braids criss-crossed in the center in characteristic Tigre style. Fatna, thinking I desired such a fashion, began to separate my hair into orderly strands and started braiding. Then, her effort finished, she held me at arm's distance to inspect her work. My hair was not too cooperative, but they were delighted that at least I was more like them. The warmth of being included and befriended relaxed me.

One thing was missing: braided hair and bracelet-clad arms needed a veil. I remembered that I had a yard of material that might do. Just that morning one of the village men had returned with my sandal. He had been to a "store" somewhere, but the store sold only tea and sugar. The man, not wishing to return empty-handed, and probably in an attempt to pacify me, had brought me a yard of multicolored striped material along with my useless sandal. A strip of material had seemed worthless to me. I had accepted it gratefully, nevertheless; it would be a souvenir of my experiences with the E.L.F. I ran inside the hut to get it and draped it over my head and shoulders. The women cupped their hands over their mouths and giggled sheepishly as I returned.

They suddenly remembered that they were in the middle of building their shelter. Together, we resumed the work. When the last mat was thrown loosely over the igloo-shaped hut, the women moved to another site several yards away to begin on another hut.

Fatna dug into a bundle of mats and long poles on the ground. The moon softened the darkening sky as she carried several large stones to a flattened area and formed a foundation for a square platform. The platform, made of narrow slats of wood bound with hides, would be the only furniture in the hut—it would serve as bed, couch, cedar chest, pantry, table, and chairs. Next she sat on her haunches, took an iron rod used for grinding coffee beans, and with a flat rock hammered a shallow hole into the ground. One of the long sticks was wedged into the hole. Two feet away she made another hole into which she placed another long stick. The frame of the hut was going up. I was invited to participate; Fatna pounded, and I wedged sticks into the holes. Her youngest child, his chunky body unsteady, wobbled over to her. He was interested more in what she could give him than in what she was doing. Letting out an angry cry, he grabbed her breast. She pulled him into her lap, and he sucked contentedly while she continued to

Left: Muslim women build a Tigre hut. *Greet Rietkerk*

Below: The igloo-shaped hut stands complete with its covering of grass mats. A hand-hewn wooden bowl sits in the doorway. *Greet Rietkerk*

pound. The circumference of sticks soon closed in and the frame took shape. I marveled at the small interior. It looked no larger than our bathroom at Ghinda. Shorter sticks tied at the top connected the curved side sticks to complete the oval sphere.

As the women threw grass mats over the frame, pinning them down and tying them with rope, several village men led by Fatna's husband began to build a shelter for the goats only several yards away from the hut. A number of the E.L.F. joined them enthusiastically. Casting their weapons to the ground, they uprooted cactus plants, thrusting them into a pile to form a barrier. A circular wall several feet high was erected; logs were placed on top to form a tepee-style structure, and the goats were herded inside.

As they worked, one of the soldiers yelled to me, saying, "This is how we do things here. We all help one another. You see, we are here to help the people."

The huts were finished. Everyone settled down to wait for the evening meal. I wandered to the storage hut, fingering the bracelets on my arms. A smile flitted across my face as I thought of the special treats the day had held despite the bitter disappointments.

The sound of plodding feet and a barrage of snorts and grunts aroused me the next morning. Rounding the path in front of the hut was a camel led by a villager. Its back swayed with a cumbersome burden. Packed on its back were several jerry cans and crates. The fuel for the helicopter had come. I wondered if the camel would not have been a more reliable means of transportation, since it seldom needed refueling.

After unloading the camel, the soldiers brought a crate into the hut and began to examine the contents. I sat enthralled as they pulled out can after can of various foods: four cans of luncheon meat, a canned beef brisket, six small cans of assorted fruit and fruit juices, six cans of soup, and a package of spaghetti. The crate also had some most unusual groceries for so remote a place: a box of refined salt, a box of tea bags, a can of olive oil, even a bottle of catsup and two rolls of toilet paper. Toilet paper! To top it off there was a canned ham. My eyes popped. We never ate ham in

Ethiopia! At Christmastime we had searched the store shelves in vain for an imported canned ham that would fit our budget. Dessert was also included: a large box of vanilla cookies. Where had the food come from? Was it was for Grant and me? Did it mean the E.L.F. expected to hold me for weeks or even months? Looking at the low prices marked on everything, I knew the food could not have been purchased from stores in Asmara. The only logical conclusion was that it had come from the American consulate for us.

Grant and I strutted about the hut all day, waiting for something else to happen. Surely something would happen. The fuel had arrived; the helicopter could fly as far as Asmara. Silence and uncertainty gnawed at our minds.

The day passed. The helicopter stood on its pad. The soldiers drummed up excuses. Adam, they said, was in charge. No one moved without his approval.

I suddenly realized who Adam was: the man who always wore the fatigue cap. I had met him at the helicopter the first day, but he had never bothered to introduce himself. Since he knew no English, Yakob had done all the talking. Adam's whereabouts was usually a mystery to me, but when he was at the village, the storage hut was his "oval office." That explained my frequent moves to the *adde*'s hut.

Supper was the usual. Berhane and Adam came to us as we were finishing. I looked at Adam closer. His stony countenance recalled pictures of Nazi officers. Although he was short, he stood erect and proud with an air that exacted respect from all who came before him. He wore a neatly tailored jacket with four pockets. The wide lapels easily could have supported a string of metals, but brass buttons alone embellished the front.

"Adam says for you to come, Grant," Berhane announced. "You're leaving."

"Yeah? What about the girl?" replied Grant.

"Just you. She stays here."

"Where are we going *this* time?" Grant asked skeptically.

"On a very short trip, then you will go back to Asmara," came the reply.

"Huh!" Grant huffed, stomping out the hut. "I'll believe that when I see it! Look, you guys, I'm getting sick and tired of this. What are you trying to do anyway? This is the last time. I'm not going to keep carting you all around these mountains! If you don't let me go this time, I'm going to get in the helicopter and leave myself. You can shoot me down if you want!"

I cringed. I would have feared being shot then. Having said it all, and too much at that, Grant stormed toward the helicopter.

Several minutes later I watched as the helicopter lifted off and headed in the opposite direction from Asmara. The moon was already assuming a prominent place in the sky. Soon it would be night.

Grant had left me for the last time.

"Wake-up, Mrs. Debbie. You will write a letter for us."

It was just past six o'clock Saturday morning, June 1. Berhane stood at the head of my cot, shaking me. There was a note of urgency in his voice.

It was not exactly good news to wake up to. Why should they want me to write another letter? Was the first letter not doing anything? A messenger would take days to carry the letter over the mountains to Ghinda, and days to return with a reply. An early release seemed hopeless.

Before I could crawl out of my sleeping bag, Berhane brought pen and pad and dictated what I should say.

"Address it to your mission and the Ethiopian government."

The Ethiopian government? Why them? They were the enemies of the E.L.F.! I shuddered to think what it could mean. Were the E.L.F. bargaining with the government for my release? Were they trying for the release of political prisoners, members of the E.L.F.? If so, my release would never materialize. I thought again about the kidnapped Tenneco men who had been held two months.

I looked down at the pad in front of me. Berhane continued with his dictation, but I did not hear him. I could think only about having to live with the E.L.F. for two months . . . or longer.

"Tell them that you are being well cared for, and that they must answer the requests quickly." Berhane's remark roused me.

"But I can't understand," I retorted. "Why is this letter going to the Ethiopian government?"

"Never mind, Mrs. Debbie. You will be released soon," was Berhane's only answer. It was *always* his answer.

I began to write, carefully noting the date and the time of writing so the mission would know how long it took to get a letter.

June 1—6:30 A.M.

To American Evangelical Mission and
   the Ethiopian Government:
The Lord continues to care for me and His Word is precious. I am
O.K. at present and continue to trust God for His plan. The E.L.F.
are caring for me and request an answer to their requests quickly if
I am to return quickly.

                    Debbie

Berhane read the letter slowly, stumbling over the words "precious" and "request." He left the hut for several minutes, then reentered.

"Mrs. Debbie, write down what foods you want to eat. Whatever you want, we will get."

"I just want to go home. The food I have here is enough. I just can't stay here long."

"Never mind," came his sterile reply.

I picked up the pen reluctantly. Eating was furthest from my mind. I could think only of Karl. I jotted down several items on the pad, including eggs and cheese for a protein-enriched diet. Berhane left the hut to give the list to Adam. Then Adam must have gone, for I did not see him for many days.

Not anxious to meet the sun's blistering morning rays, but even less anxious to stay inside the dingy hut, I strolled outside. Scanning the wide island plateau, I looked for and found a flat rock to sit on. I settled down, facing westward. Scattered cacti, their odd shapes reminiscent of a Picasso sculpture, flecked the brown mountainside. Herds of goats also dotted the scene, their bleating cries echoing through the valley below me. Closer by, a woman bent low to gather the stalks of stubby thornbushes. A large acacia tree, boughs laden with leaves, graced the banks of an empty riverbed below. The old gnarled tree shaded withered grass and stunted cedars. It was the largest tree I had seen in that part of Ethiopia. The people of Eritrea had cut down the trees with no plan to replant. A ruthless sun, sandy soil, and drained riverbeds were grim reminders of a land once lush with forests and wildlife.

I longed to be seated on the riverbank under the tree's protective shield. It reminded me of the Old Testament prophet Elijah. During a three-year drought in his country, he lived on the bank of a brook. There God ministered to him and provided his needs daily. Although the land yielded no food and none was available, God gave food to Elijah through the mouth of a raven. Meat and bread were brought to him twice daily. I marveled that God had met Elijah's needs so spectulary. But that was many, many years ago. Was God still the same today? Could He still meet my needs? Was He really the same God today as He was yesterday?

I cried out to Him, listing my needs. Things I had once considered essential I no longer needed. I needed only Him—the reassurance of His control over all things, the reassurance of His love for me, the ability, given by Him, to accept what I may yet have to face. I pleaded with God to minister to me as He had to Elijah.

My prayer was broken by a squalling cry high in the sky. Circling directly overhead was a raven! Craning my neck, I watched it soar. Tears flooded my eyes as I looked beyond the black outstretched wings to the sweeping clouds and lifted my thankful heart to God for such a powerful demonstration of His love for me, for such evidence of His continued care. He was the very same God that had provided for Elijah, and I began to see the many ways He was caring for me.

When I left the rock to return to the hut, for example, my sandal was fixed by a young soldier, who, upon seeing the flopping strap, pulled a nail from the storage hut door and secured the strap to the sole. Later, Sayeed came to me and with his toothless grin, handed me a bar of pink soap—to make me feel nice, he added. How I longed to wash!

God even gave me something to keep my mind and hands busy that day. As I scanned the burlap sacks filled with grain in the hut, my mind stopped short. Burlap . . . at home I had started some embroidery on colored burlap. I could get a needle from Sayeed. The day before I had seen him patching a shirt torn on a thornbush, and there was sure to be an empty burlap sack somewhere. I could separate the tie string from the sack for thread.

I searched for an empty sack; none was available. Next I thought of the first-aid kit. Opening the lid quickly, I found it: a muslin triangular bandage.

I was all set. The metal kit served as a drawing board, and taking the pen still in my pocket from Monday morning rounds, I sketched a verse onto the bandage. It was a verse I had repeated over and over since the day of my capture. Karl and I had frequently sung it together:

I SOUGHT

THE LORD

AND HE HEARD ME AND

DELIVERED ME

FROM ALL MY

FEARS.

PS. 34

MAY 27, 1974

Having borrowed a needle and begged heavy thread from Sayeed, I began to embroider, using a split stitch. Soon, however, I used up the short piece of thread. I went to the old *adde*'s hut with my problem and showed her my unfinished work. She inspected it with amazement as she fingered the letters and then rummaged through her belongings, finding everything but thread.

Her own clothes showed that she was unaccustomed to mending. After a few more "hut calls," I obtained more thread and continued my project until evening.

With darkness descending, I thought of visiting my new friends again. My first stop was Fatna's hut. As I approached the entrance, I could see her body rocking rhythmically as her outstretched arms bore down on the stone she used for grinding corn. Then taking a handful of the flour she had just ground, she sifted it through her fingers, threw it back onto the grinding stone, and continued. I greeted her, and we kissed each other's hands in the customary Muslim manner. She begged me to enter and sit down. She sat next to me and for a few moments just stared and grinned.

Again my long straight hair fascinated her, and she pulled her fingers through it. Then, acting on impulse, she did something that would have astonished any other Muslim women who might be watching. She pulled the faded red veil off her head. A sea of tightly woven braids fell around her face and down her back. At the top of her head sat a revered piece of jewelry: a ball-shaped piece of metal that crowned the head of every married Muslim woman. It was to be seen and admired only by her husband. Acting like a six-year-old with pigtails, Fatna shook her head happily back and forth to make her braids fly in all directions. At the sound of men's voices outside, her grin faded abruptly. With a look of embarrassment she pulled the veil back swiftly over her head just as the men entered the hut.

The next hut to visit was one I had never been to before. I felt a bit awkward about visiting someone I did not even know, but the friendliness of the other women encouraged me, and I decided to walk over. As I neared, I noticed a woman strolling at the far side of the hut. I thought it rather peculiar that the hut was huddled in a remote corner, and I wondered too why I had never seen the woman before. She had not socialized with the others. Her head hung low; her face was hidden by her veil.

"*Salaam,*" I greeted her.

Looking up, she returned the greeting and then invited me inside. Quiet embers in the firepit told me her supper was over. Her hut was strangely bare and unusually neat. A wooden bowl was set carefully with a straw-and-mud pot in one corner next to the grinding stone. A goatskin bag used for making buttermilk was stretched across two poles near the entrance flap.

We chatted for awhile since she knew some Tigrinya. My vocabulary, limited to brief greetings and simple medical terms, made conversation difficult. I learned her name was Jimma. As I left, she invited me to visit again.

Returning to the storage hut, I dropped to my cot. The hut was filled with men sipping coffee. I thought about Fatna and how much more comfortable I was in her presence. She had become my friend. But those men were my captors. My eyes shifted from their faces to their guns. All I could see was the wrong they had done, the greed for authority, power, and political rule. All I could see was the masked man confronting me in the hospital corridor. All I could see was Anna, thrown backward on the rocks as a bullet ripped out her life. How could I love them?

On Sunday, June 2, my bitterness waned as I went outside to sit on my rock overlooking "Elijah's tree." My thoughts centered on the Sunday before when Karl had preached on loneliness.

As I reflected upon the sermon, his voice echoed through the valleys. "I am not alone, because the Father is with me" were Jesus' words to His disciples shortly before His death. Jesus' words also spoke to me as I meditated on God's comfort in loneliness. I wrote my thoughts in a notebook tucked in my pocket and once used for memos during hospital rounds.

> In my loneliness from my husband—
> That one ordained by You to be
> My head, my companion, my *joy*—
> Give me Your comfort, God.
> So often would I run to him before
> For comfort;
> Now You are teaching me in his absence
> To run to You.

And would You grant union again
So that having learned what it means
To be comforted by You,
We may comfort others.

When I returned to the hut some time later Sayeed held out a piece of folded white material resembling cheesecloth.

"This *netsula* is for you," he said with Berhane again interpreting. "You need something soft. You can put it inside your sleeping bag, and it will be soft for you to sleep on."

I was touched by their expression of concern for me. The downy smoothness of the material felt feminine. I may have had greasy, stringy hair, a body badly in need of a bubblebath, and a dingy-gray uniform stained with perspiration and smudged with dirt, but as I opened the cloth and draped it over my head it made me feel like a woman again.

Later that evening I wore the veil as I made what was becoming routine visits. I particularly wanted to see Jimma again. Her hut was dark, and I wondered if she were home. Peering around the entrance flap, I found her hunched next to the fire. She welcomed me in. I had brought her several of the cookies from the grocery crate. Her sallow cheeks dimpled with a smile, and in a soft, mousy voice she bade me to sit down.

For a time I just sat and watched the flames dance in the shallow firepit and thought about Jimma. Earlier I had asked Berhane about her husband, since I had never seen her with a family. I was told no one seemed to know who he was. I realized she was an outcast, rejected by her society because she did not have what was most treasured by the Muslim community: children. How oppressive life must be for a nomadic woman! A mere extension of her husband and children, she could never have her own individuality. If she could give no children, she was nothing.

I longed to talk to Jimma about the tender way Christ dealt with women, even those spurned by their society. He freed them first from their self-inflicted oppression rooted in their rejection of God.

He made them completed individuals. No longer were they hidden in the shadows of others or in the darkness of their own sin. I could only gesture to Jimma and repeat a few words. How would she ever know?

As I rose to leave a half hour later, I squeezed her hand. She asked me to stay for coffee. I looked at her shabby dress, her empty pots, and her empty grain barrel. She had no one to provide for her. She started to call one of the village children to borrow some sugar, but I knew she would not be able to pay it back. I declined her offer, promising to visit again.

Monday morning Berhane interrupted my embroidery work to suggest that my uniform be washed right away. Washed! I looked at it. How could it be washed? And it was all I had to wear! He explained that a young village girl could wash it down at the water hole.

I refused his plan. I could not be sure I would ever get it back, nor did I know how I would maintain any semblance of modesty without it. Besides, I kept telling myself, I would not be there much longer.

But Berhane insisted. Apparently my filthiness bothered him more than it did me. He handed me a clean knit tee-shirt of Sayeed's to wear while my uniform was being washed, and also suggested that I wrap the yard of striped material around my waist. I had to give in, and taking advantage of Berhane's offer, I asked for a bowl of water for a bath.

After the men left the hut, I donned my new costume and secured the ankle-length "skirt" around my waist with a safety pin I found in the first-aid kit. When I emerged from the hut, Sayeed told me I looked beautiful wearing a long wraparound like the Muslim women.

Berhane handed me a small bowl of water that appeared as though someone else had already bathed with it. Taking it to a cluster of cacti, I cast a surveilling eye in all directions before partly undressing. I usually had a curious entourage of village children wherever I went and found it especially annoying when my hiding places for privacy were always being discovered. Just squatting to take care of my normal, everyday needs was enough to distract children from playing as they pressed for a closer look.

I began to wash with the soap Sayeed had given me. I had no washcloth, but I still had the towel given to me the first afternoon following the cloudburst. I had protected it carefully and found it useful as a pillow, a headscarf to shield against the hot sun, and a light blanket for afternoon snoozes. After the sudsing and once-over rinse, I washed my underwear in the murky leftover water and hung it to dry over a cactus.

Returning, I found my uniform draped over the side of the hut and dripping with water. Struck by my unusual opportunity to bathe and wash in the wilderness, I sat down with my notebook, thankful that the men did not disturb me from this form of express-ing myself.

> Thank You God that though
> I have only dirty water
> To wash in—
> You have reminded me
> As I look at the earth below me
> That my heart is washed pure
> *White* as this glistening marble rock
> Beneath my feet.
> I am clean in the
> Righteousness of Jesus!

My uniform had dried by evening. As I slipped it on and pulled it over my abdomen before going to bed, I wondered how long it would fit me.

The sun had not yet broken over the eastern slope of mountains before light filtered through the cracks in the log roof. I heard rustling at the foot of my bed. Squinting through the darkness, I saw outlines of two figures packing a box. Outside the hut I heard the click of hoofs and the snort of a mule. I turned over in my sleeping bag, wondering what it all meant. Could it mean my

This Muslim woman nurses her son. Often women nurse their children until three or four years of age. Because they fail to give them other nutritious food, many are malnourished. Note the lump on top of the mother's head. Hidden under her veil is her honored piece of jewelry.

release? I strained to hear any word of instruction.

"Let's go, Mrs. Debbie. We're moving today." It was Berhane speaking.

Moving! I could barely splurt out the words, "Are we going back to Ghinda?"

My question was ignored. The men piled the one large cooking pot, a small teapot, food, and other items into a rope bag.

"Are we going to Ghinda?" I asked louder, and then held my breath for the answer.

"I'm sure that you will understand that I had to open the letters and read them . . . Your wife is well." Haile fumbled in a soft, distinguished voice to excuse himself after he had handed me the three letters on Friday morning, May 31.

I knew that they would have been opened the previous evening. My fingers trembled as I received them. First I read the one to the mission from Debbie.

May 28—1:00 P.M.

To American Evangelical Mission
  and the American Consulate.

I'm in an unknown place held by the Eritrean Liberation Front. I'm well physically and mentally and continually praising God. The E.L.F. have stated that they want a supply of medications in exchange for me and that they will release me when they have the supplies. You should contact the E.L.F. within 48 hours. May God be with you as He is with me. Psalm 91.

With a sigh of relief I passed the letter to Jim. My greatest concern was lifted: Debbie was alive and had been filled with the presence and comfort of God. As He had met my every need, so had He provided for her. Forty-eight hours had long passed since the letter was written, but I thought that the E.L.F. letter would clarify some points. I read it immediately.

Date 5/29/74
ERITREAN LIBERATION FRONT
ERITREAN LIBERATION ARMY
To Evangelical Mission (American)
& U.S. Consul General Asmara
Mrs. Debbie American Evangelical Mission Ghinda Hospital Nurse is by now in the hands of E.L.F. For her release you should have to contact us quickly and discuss with us about the case. And we will explain for you why the reason we have done all the action in the Hospital that happens Date 5/27/74. Before that, we want to remind you that if we hear in the news given us the title of Rebels, it is very risky in her life. We want the Broadcast to give us our real name "ERITREAN LIBERATION FRONT." Don't accept any letters if it didn't have an official seal.
Executive Committee.

I reacted immediately to three things. First, Debbie would be kept alive; they wanted something for her. Second, their threat on her life if we did not use their proper title probably presented no real danger. Third, the difficulty was in making quick contact. We had tried for four days to make any contact at all.

Finally I opened a second envelope—in it was the third letter, addressed to me.

Dearest Karl,   May 28
The Lord is our strength and our salvation . . . I am praying God will be glorified—I am praying for you. Please be assured of my constant and growing love.
Please encourage a quick response to the requests.
To His Praise and in His love,
Deb

My face flushed and my ears tingled. It was the first letter I had received from Debbie since before our marriage three years earlier, but it could be compared with none of the others. Seeing the

74

handwriting reminded me again of her love, of our relationship, and of the impossible miles that separated us. Her words encouraged me because I knew we shared the same love. I tore my mind away from Debbie in order to make a quick response.

Jim and I went immediately to the S.I.M. to obtain the mission stationery and stamp. The seal at the bottom of the letters just received meant "official," and we knew our reply had to be equally official. Haile would await our reply, but it had to be back without delay. Neither Jim nor I talked about the letters until we left Haile's office, but when we did, our thoughts ran exactly parallel.

On the way home I formulated a reply. I had to know how many medicines, what kind, and where we should take them. When we arrived at the S.I.M. compound, Greet and Art were there. We shared the news excitedly and then sat down for collective wisdom on my reply. All the other missionaries also gathered and listened as I read first the letters we had received, and then, without waiting for their response, my intended reply.

Dead silence. No one spoke. Something was amiss. Then slowly, agonizingly, they made me see my error: We could have no assurance that Debbie would be released once we had met the E.L.F. demands. To acquiese to such demands for blood money would most certainly spawn further demands. All hope for future missionary work would be destroyed. Any missionary would become a prime target for repeated E.L.F. assaults.

The decision to take a hard and determined stand brought the nagging thought that I was betraying my own wife. If I did not care, who would? At once I saw what was really at stake. Either I would trust God to deliver Debbie, or I would give in to the demands and trust my own power. The last few days of agony and delivery had taught me how powerless I was. I possessed no record of deliverances, nor had I any idea of how to persuade the E.L.F. to do what they said they would do, much less *make* them do what I wanted. My confidence could be only in what God could do, not in the ransom that I might pay. Christ had already ransomed Debbie; His promise was that He would care for her.

The point was made; I drafted another response and read it to those seated with me.

May 31, 1974
10:30 A.M.

Eritrean Liberation Front
Executive Committee

I have received your letter stating demands for the return of Mrs. Debbie. No demands will be considered until Mrs. Debbie is released.

Your letter of her came to me only at 10:00 this morning, because contacts have been slow in giving it to me. Best contact is via shumes in Ghinda and Afabet.

The only way that we have or will refer to you is by Eritrean Liberation Front.

Mr. Karl Dortzbach

The letter was approved heartily. Since we had no assurance that Haile would actually get our letter to the E.L.F., I wrote three originals: one for Haile, one for the shumes in Ghinda, and one for those in Afabet. We felt that one of the three should reach its destination.

Later in the afternoon I visited The Alayn where the Tenneco representatives stayed. The information about Debbie was popping out of me, and I wanted to share it with them. I was also upset and wanted to find out what "the Major" knew about the letters. Obviously, he too had read them the night before, and it seemed likely that Tenneco had heard from him.

I went to the third floor and rapped on door 327. Mr. Birchal answered. He was a middle-aged man, and he puffed nervously on his pipe. Undoubtedly, he was suffering from two months of tension and pressure following attempts to release his company's men. When I asked him if he knew about our letters, he denied it firmly, but was glad we had *some* word. He had been with "the Major" at ten-thirty the night before, and had tried unsuccessfully to contact him all morning. Mr. Birchal wanted to help however he could.

With that he burst into a long explanation of all his difficulties, and I was amazed that the man still had his sanity. He had trusted in people that double-crossed him. He had sent letters and supplies, but no answer ever came back. Finally he had sent another company helicopter for a clandestine meeting to rescue the men. "The Major" had promised him that that time everything would work. Instead Anna was dead, Debbie was kidnapped, and he had lost another man.

"What can I do?" he cried out. "I've told 'the Major' I would give anything—three million dollars, my own life, *anything*. But I haven't even had a letter saying what they want."

I cringed—if anyone knew how much money he was talking about, I would never see Debbie.

"Mr. Birchal," I interrupted, "do you know how much we will pay for Debbie?"

"No."

"Not one thin dime!" His eyes bulged. I continued, "If you give money or even promise it, her life won't last longer than it takes you to spend a nickel! We don't have any money to pay! All we can do is trust that God will use the pressure of all the shumes and news releases about a nurse's murder and a kidnapped pregnant woman." I turned and left without any of my questions answered.

When Saturday morning, the first of June, came, I wondered if Haile had delivered the letter to the E.L.F. the day before. Martin Katschall, a forty-year veteran of the S.I.M., was to fly to Afabet that day and take a copy of our letter to the shumes there. They could get it to the proper leaders. Before leaving, however, he wanted all cooperating missions to write a letter of protest to the shumes.

A general letter with official stamps and signatures of four missions would impress the village shumes and hopefully cause them to act quicker in finding information. Participating in the discussion at the S.I.M. that morning was another helicopter pilot who flew for Tenneco. He was a kind of quasi-official representative. We had to make it clear to the shumes, Tenneco, and the E.L.F. that no money would be paid.

Martin Katschall as the penman drafted the letter. His lengthy missionary experience enabled him to relate to the shumes.

1 June 1974

To the Elders of the People of Eritrea
Dear Sirs:
    Greetings in the name of our God who is merciful, good and compassionate.
    All missions located below wish to protest in the strongest possible way the cowardly violence of men who kill women and take pregnant women to endanger the birth of their firstborn sons. We also strongly protest the taking of innocent men to hold for ransom when they come with peace in their hearts and no weapons in their hands. . . .

The letter continued to explain that all mission activity would cease until the hostages were released. When the letter was completed, and each mission had read its copy, the ceremonious sealing and signing of the letter began. One might have thought it was the Declaration of Independence. Actually it was a declaration of dependence, for all of us felt that God would use the shumes and their pressure on the E.L.F. to answer our prayer for Debbie's release. Hopefully, the shumes would be able to turn the minds of her ruthless captors.

When Martin Katschall had taken the letters to Afabet and returned, he described the details of his trip, but even he did not know how much help the shumes could give us. He had gone to the mission station where a large group of the shumes were assembled. In true Muslim tradition a few stood to give their condolences on behalf of the group; the least important first, then the most influential. They promised to help us in whatever way possible. After several minutes of discussion Martin read an Arabic translation of the general mission letter. It brought grave faces and amens from all the shumes who knew its meaning well. All mission activities would cease: the village clinic would be vacant, the new retaining dam would remain unfinished and crops would not be watered, the new wells would remain capped with their windmills unassembled. Although the shumes were sympathetic and understood the reason for such drastic action, it still hurt, and their faces reflected that hurt.

After another round of talking Martin had placed my letter of reply on the table along with the mission letter, saying that they had to be delivered to the E.L.F. The letters were dynamite. Everyone hung back. Although all had promised to help, no one dared go forward in public to take the letters lest he be immediately identified as the courier.

Not until Martin had begun to talk with individual shumes after the meeting was information disclosed. The most significant thing he learned was that Debbie had recently been taken to a desert village some forty or fifty miles southwest of Afabet. An incredible network of messengers and lookouts had tallied the exact route, the number of stops between points, and even the number of donkey changes made. She was well and being treated with respect. Her release would be soon, for at that very time three important sheikhs were traveling to the village. Martin had had his back to the table, and when he turned around to talk with someone else, the letters were missing.

We talked among ourselves and felt certain that Debbie was with the five Tenneco men. Debbie had been kidnapped for five days, five days had elapsed before we could send a single reply. How much longer would it take? Could the shumes actually obtain her release after only one letter? Did the combined mission shutdown apply enough pressure on the E.L.F.? Everything possible was done. The missions were risking their reputation and influence. Sheikhs gambled with their lives on our behalf, and the shumes would certainly carry our letters to the E.L.F.

Sunday morning, June 2, came and for the first time I began to think about other things than Monday's kidnapping—things like preaching and teaching. I had preached every Sunday during the past year but that Sunday was different. I would not travel to the nearby Ethiopian Naval Base for Bible classes. I would not be preaching in the English service at the hospital. Instead I would be listening and learning from someone else.

I attended a worship service in Asmara, where the preacher expounded the familiar Psalm 23. As he spoke about the care of the Good Shepherd for His sheep, I wondered if Debbie had water. If she had, it was probably stagnant and was transported in moldy goatskins. She had worn the same clothes for six days and nights in the sweltering heat—and God cared? As the service ended, I leafed through my Bible. I had not used that particular Bible since the week before when I preached in Ghinda. My eyes were caught by a piece of paper—my sermon notes for that earlier service. The contents had lain forgotten. I read the title again: "Lonely?" Yes.

I read my description of loneliness. I felt it. People thronged around me. Everyone advised me. Encouragement grew like flowers in the spring, but the seat next to me was empty. Frustration and fear fermented inside me, distilling depression. Debbie's assuring, attentive listening was gone. The warm touch of her hand on mine was missing.

I read the sermon text almost unwillingly, afraid that I would find an answer that did not seem to be working: "In me you have peace. . . ." I wish. "In this world you have tribulation. . . ." Obviously. "But take courage. I have overcome the world." Jesus' words promised hope and peace in His victory over sin and its death penalty. That victory was the power for living, power available only when I asked His forgiveness for trying to rely upon my own strength. I had convinced myself of that power the week before, but it had escaped me. I prayed for it again:

"Father, I don't know what to do . . . show me. I can't do what I know I should do . . . help me."

Later in the afternoon Bob Perry telephoned from the consulate to say that Birchal had left mysteriously early that morning. A note he wrote indicated he had flown with "the Major" to a town called Agordat. His exact purpose was not revealed; Birchal had said only that he would return that same day with at least the nurse and maybe another hostage. Agordat was in the same area where the shumes reported Debbie to be.

My hopes mounted instantly. Since Debbie's capture Tenneco had talked about a show of good faith from the E.L.F. They demanded that one or two captives be released before further negotiations would be made. Would Debbie return with Birchal as a show of good faith? Impatiently, we awaited his return.

Five o'clock came and went without a message from Birchal. Six o'clock; not even a telephone call. The airport closed to private planes. What was to have been a quick one-day operation in an E.L.F. hotbed stretched on indefinitely. We concluded that Birchal had invested the day on another airy promise from "the Major" and hoped he would not be the seventh Tenneco hostage.

Monday, June 3, we waited for a call. Perhaps our skepticism was wrong and Debbie would be with Birchal. Five-thirty found Jim, Bob, and me searching the sky for a small plane. At six-thirty a dot appeared on the western horizon. Minutes later the plane landed and taxied to the hangar. When the propeller stopped, Birchal climbed out . . . alone.

My heart sank again. Birchal's promises were worse than nothing. The four of us went to the consulate where Birchal related his story.

"The Major" had actually gone alone to the area where the captives were. He had almost reached them.

"And then," Birchal said, "he was stopped by some men with guns—they identified themselves as E.L.F. They knew what he had come for, but they demanded to see the receipt. 'No receipt, no passage,' they had told him."

I groaned. Anyone who had ever spent more than a month in Ethiopia knew that receipts were for only one thing: money. Every official cash transaction had to have a receipt.

"Did you pay any money?" I asked.

"No," Birchal answered me insistently. "I don't know anything about a receipt or what it would have been for. They're crazy. They're all crazy."

We hoped Tenneco would stop negotiations and let us try things our way. We wanted to allow the shumes time to work. We wanted the love, kindness, and help shown by the missions throughout the years to touch the E.L.F. leaders. Birchal's report of being foiled for lack of a "receipt" was disturbing. Whether or not money had actually passed we did not know. What we did know was that the E.L.F. thought the money had been paid. Tenneco's presence in the area had confirmed that to them. The E.L.F. confused our mission with Tenneco because we both sought the release of all captives. It was evident, however, that our solution was very different. A joint effort to free all captives was no longer feasible. We feared that the Tenneco actions had endangered Debbie's life because it gave the E.L.F. a false hope that ransom would be paid.

Monday had been declared a "day of prayer" to petition for the captives' release. We especially prayed that Tenneco's attempts in Agordat would somehow produce Debbie, or at least some hope of her release. Several people tried to assure me, saying, "The Lord told me Debbie would be released today." How the Lord told them remained a mystery, but I did know that in the Bible Jesus promised, "Ask and you will receive that your joy may be made full." I asked, and during the day many others asked. But when Monday night came, I still had not received.

Tuesday morning brought no change. Surely the shumes in Afabet could have reached Debbie's desert village by then, but our letters produced nothing.

Satan pounded away at me. I knew the battle was within myself . . . "God had promised," I would say to myself, and I would answer, "Yeah, but He didn't do it, did He?" That drove me back to read the promise again . . . Jesus never said *when* He would answer. Even then, the answer might be to give strength to bear the disappointment.

82

Early after lunch Bob Perry telephoned me again.

"Grant was released in Ghinda this morning," he said. "Can you come to the office to meet him?"

My heart skipped a beat. I knew Grant was the helicopter pilot with Debbie. He would be able to tell us about her. Perhaps she was close behind and would be released that day . . . or the next. I found Ben Motis, and together we drove to the consulate.

Ben was the missionary in charge of the Afabet station. If Debbie were near there, he would be the most help since he knew the terrain, the villages, and many of the men. He had often been a tremendous encouragement and help to me with his calmness and sure confidence in God. I could benefit from his example of not jumping to hasty ideas or conclusions. As we sped to the consulate, I twitched with excitement.

Once inside the office, we introduced ourselves to Grant who told me right away, "Your wife's O.K." I was as surprised at his appearance as he probably was at mine. I had not expected to see a pilot in long hair, jeans, and tennis shoes. But I must have fit his image of a missionary even less in my bell-bottom levis, sandals, and bushy beard.

I was bursting with curiosity since he obviously had not been mistreated. It gave me hope for Debbie—but why had he been released? The answer emerged slowly.

"The E.L.F. told me I could go because I hadn't been part of a plan to exploit the country—that's the charge made against the other men," he said, puffing vigorously on his cigarette.

He commented first on one event and then on another as though it were difficult to know where to begin. He filled us in on what he knew of Debbie: she had been in a small village as of the previous Friday, May 31, was playing with the children and women, and seemed in good spirits.

"Did you know about Anna's murder?" I asked.

"No," he said with amazement. "I didn't find out until I got to Asmara. I don't think Debbie knew either. She couldn't have known—she was too calm."

I had wondered whether she knew. If she did not, I was sure her own plight would be easier to take. Still, her calmness could be understood: the Lord could have given her peace in spite of the trauma.

"Where is she now?" I asked. "Near Ghinda or Afabet?"

"I don't know the names of villages," he said, "but is there a topographical map around here?"

Bob Perry produced one. With a mental record of his flying time, speed, direction, and elevation, Grant traced the journey on the map, starting at Ghinda. They had flown about thirty minutes north and set down in what looked like a banana grove. Awaiting them there had been several men with supplies. Next they had flown north by west for another thirty minutes. That area on the map appeared much closer to Afabet than to Ghinda, yet still some distance from Afabet.

The description of the village and Grant's days there helped us to answer some more questions. His travel back had taken three days by foot and donkey. The worst thing that happened to him in captivity had been a fall off the donkey that still left him painfully stiff.

"I could have done better walking," he remarked contemptuously, "but they wouldn't let me."

When we asked why the hospital had been raided, Grant gave us the dubious reply they had given him.

"All they told me was that they went to the hospital to get a doctor so that he could test water holes for cholera." He went on to explain that near one water hole the E.L.F. had allegedly found small vials with "cholera" printed on them. They knew the government had sent a group of men to a desert area; hence they charged the government with poisoning the water holes.

We knew of a similar report transmitted from Baghdad that the *mission* had poisoned the water holes. "Cholera" vials probably had been found, but they were left by a vaccination team sent by the Public Health Ministry to an area called Sheib. There the team had inoculated hundreds *against* cholera. Few people understood that the vaccination was not totally effective. Thus when people died who had been injected, the suspicion of poisoning aroused many of the villagers.

Grant brought no message about Debbie's release; no lines of communication had been set up. Even the reason for the hospital raid remained a mystery. The cholera charge failed to explain Anna's murder and Debbie's capture. Grant's release had solved only two questions: that of his own release, and that Debbie was well as of the day when he had last seen her. He knew nothing of the letters we wrote, but he thought ransom demands would be made. Debbie had not been released with Grant for a reason, a reason not yet clear.

On Wednesday, June 5, a country man clad in dirty-gray muslin came into our hospital. He held a three-feet-long walking stick horizontally on his shoulders. After handing a folded-up piece of paper to one of the workers standing guard inside, he plodded right out. The worker, upon opening it, saw at once the Eritrean Liberation Front seal displayed clearly at the lower corner and that it was a letter addressed to the mission. Fearful of illegal possession of an E.L.F. letter, he ran to a nearby army guard without considering what might happen to the letter before we received it.

When the letter reached an army commander, he immediately sent word back to a hospital worker, requesting that someone secure permission from us to be courier of the letter. Ramadan, another hospital worker, rushed to us in Asmara.

"A letter came to the hospital!" he relayed with wide eyes. "The worker gave it to the army—stupids, they should know better— and the army told me to come and get permission from you to bring it here. I have come just now."

His words were electrifying. Six days had passed since the last letter—six days of waiting, hoping, and praying. The arrival of another letter rekindled my impatience. Quickly, I wrote a letter to designate Ramadan as our courier.

"They won't give it to me," he said doubtfully. "I don't think so." And shaking his head, he headed for Ghinda with the permission in hand.

Two hours later he telephoned to confirm his prophetic words.

"They say they have no auto to come in to Asmara, and they won't send the letter with me." Disgust flamed his voice.

An older sister carries her brother on her back to the clinic. Often older children take care of the younger siblings.

CHAPTER 4

"Just stay there in bed, Mrs. Debbie. When we're ready we'll call you," announced Berhane. "We're moving to a different place today."

I buried myself in my sleeping bag. "Oh, God," I cried, "how can I keep on like this? I know nothing—where I'm going, where I am, what I will be doing. I can't stand not knowing." I began to sob. It was nine days since I had been kidnapped.

The mule was packed. Berhane called me to come. I crawled out of my sleeping bag, smoothed my uniform which I wore day and night, and left the hut. The sleeping bag was draped over the cargo-laden mule. I mounted the animal, straddling a leg on either side. Oh, for a pair of jeans! But the yard of striped material would have to do. I spread it out over my knees. Since the early air was chilly, I draped the white veil over my head, shoulders, and arms.

A stick landed on the mule's hindquarters, and we started off. Berhane, his rifle high on his shoulder, pioneered the way and also acted as sentinel to warn of approaching danger. Bekeet, Fatna's husband, led the mule, halter rope in one hand and rifle in the other. Sayeed, his red bandana clearly visible from a distance, took up the rear with another soldier. I sat the most conspicuous of all —a foreign woman draped in white, sitting high on a mule and being marched out of the village, destination unknown, reason unknown.

All the huts were dark and still. It was too early for signs of life. I turned to look at Fatna's hut, hoping she would be hovering in the shadows. I wanted a last glimpse of her. But I saw only her hut, that humble structure of stick and straw that I had helped to build. My eyes drifted to the dwelling in the outskirts of the village. Jimma would have spent the night alone again, not far from huts still crowded with sleepers. I wondered how long she would remain forgotten. Would she ever find acceptance? Her forlorn face haunted me. Again I pictured the furrows of despair as she hung her head.

Then I thought of the children, always to be found in places I did not want them: where I bathed, where I ran to cry in outbursts of despondency, wherever I yearned for privacy. In spite of their intrusion, I had enjoyed them. Once several of them had come to me as I sat on a rock and with open palms offered me several kernels of corn. We had sat side by side eating the kernels together. I had often thought of interesting them in a game but was never sure how to go about it. That chance would be gone forever.

I waved to the village as the mule began its descent to the riverbed. The huts faded from view.

Flies swarmed around my face. I could taste them. They clung persistently to my eyelids and nested into the corners. They roosted on my lips and hid in strands of my hair. Fanning my face did not help. Veiling my face did not help. Finally I just left them alone.

I felt angry. Angry about the flies . . . Angry about being spread out over the top of a mule as a spectacle . . . Angry about the unannounced move . . . Angry about being forced to leave my new friends . . . Angry about having no control over what was happening.

I felt fearful. Fearful I might be taken to a desolate mountain peak . . . to a desert hideout . . . to a deserted place for easy disposal —for hyenas to eat?

Our early morning journey continued. We passed several clusters of huts with children scurrying around them. Camels curled their legs beneath them and settled in the sand, chomping on their cuds. Children stopped their play and lingered at a distance to watch the parade pass.

Leaving the dry riverbed, we began to ascend a steep rocky hill. Bekeet guided the mule carefully, zigzagging a path around boulders, rock slides, thornbushes, and stunted cedars.

I wondered why there was no word from anyone since I had left Ghinda. Where was Karl? Probably he had left Ghinda, but what then? I doubted that he would have left the country without me, at least not so soon. Were all the other missionaries gone? I hoped the Den Hartogs had left for the States. If it really were Gil the E.L.F. wanted, it was better that he leave. Maybe the Miners had left to return home too. They were due for furlough anyway. Had Sandra, another missionary nurse, as well as Greet and the Steltzers all gone to Kenya until things would be safe, until plans could be made for the future?

Karl and I had visited Nairobi on our vacation the previous January and experienced quite a culture shock. Out of the flat grasslands, the home of cheetahs, giraffes, and lions, loomed the jagged skyline of a city more Western than African. I had not seen skyscrapers since we left New York.

I looked about me: my mule was hardly a Mercedes-Benz zipping through the streets of Nairobi, and the huts lying in the distance scraped only the ground, the sky far from them. Such different worlds.

Into what world was I being led? Slowly, we mounted the brink of the hill and then began a steeper climb. The mule buckled under its load as the path grew more treacherous. I dug my legs deeper into its sides and thrust my body forward during the near-vertical ascent. All the men had gone on ahead, leaving Bekeet and me to wend our way up. The flat mountaintop gradually opened before me. I looked for a village. There was none.

In a far corner Berhane and Sayeed were resting in a comfortable spot. Next to them stood an abandoned teepee-style shelter assembled from logs piled one against the other. The shelter was not far from a fire pit of scattered ashes surrounded by three square stones blackened on one side. I had seen several such shelters dotting the hillsides and speculated that they were shepherd huts, offering a protection from the sun.

Berhane rose to gather sticks. He had brought a hot coal in a tin can from camp. Placing it on top of the kindling, he fanned vigorously. Teatime! It would be a welcome interlude, since we had left without breakfast and had been traveling one hour.

Berhane instructed me to get down off the mule. Then Sayeed spoke:

"This is where we will stay until Adam comes. When Adam comes, you will go."

"Here?" I gasped. "What is there here? Nothing. No one. When will Adam come?"

They did not know. We had left the village, they explained, because the old *adde* was sick.

Crazy, I thought. What were the real reasons.

So the mountaintop was to be my new home. I started to investigate. The hut was small, smaller even than Fatna's mat hut. The dirt floor was no more than ten feet in diameter, and the only place one could stand upright was in the center. The ground was relatively smooth, but Sayeed swept out the stones to make it smoother. He then removed the ground cloth from his knapsack, laid it out, placed my sleeping bag over it, and beckoned me to lie down and rest. I did so gratefully. Meanwhile, Berhane finished making tea and brought it to the hut.

I thought more about the move. Were the E.L.F. afraid of being discovered? Had the Ethiopian army been spotted in pursuit of us? Was that only the beginning of early morning moves to confuse our followers and ward them off?

"Bekeet will go and get your cot and bring it here." Berhane broke into my thoughts. Get my cot? Back at the village? Strange that he should travel all the way back there. It would be an improvement, though, over the hard ground. Less chance, too, of meeting up with a snake if I were off the ground. I recoiled as I remembered a python twelve feet long that Greet and I once had encountered on a path while trekking to visit a family. I remembered, too, that one day Berhane, in futile attempts to ease my fanatical fear of snakes, had told me to "never mind"—he saw snakes every day, and they never had bothered him.

With nothing else to do, I roamed outside, and since my guards did not restrict me I sought acquaintance with my new home. The brilliant morning sun with its cheering rays had replaced the nippy air. We were settled on a small depression between two larger plateaus. Meandering over the plateau just behind the hut, I viewed the distant mountains to place my bearings. For a time during our early morning journey I had been able to keep a sense of direction. (That fact would have amazed Karl, I mused. He knew he could always trust me to be wrong about directions.) I had become confused, however, during the zigzag ascent. I looked for the riverbed. Several cleared sandy patches indicated its location. A trail of smoke was coming from a group of huts also far below—mere specks in the barren wasteland. It was the village with the camels that we had passed.

From that landmark I continued my gaze along the route I thought we had taken. Almost directly south from where I stood, my eyes settled upon another dome-shaped structure. The plateau held several other huts; one was larger and more prominent than the others. That was it! It seemed miles away. My eyes shifted to follow the course the helicopter used in approaching that village. All the events of the week before loomed in my mind. How unreal —and yet I could almost hear the whirl of the helicopter.

I slumped down on a small rock. The many deceptive sounds that entangled my mind tormented me with the expectation of seeing my rescuers. I relieved the pain of discouragement by writing in my notebook:

> There are so many sounds like
> The blades of a helicopter
> Coming for rescue:
> The tail of the morning wind,

The crackling of flames over the fire,
The bubbling soup in the pot.

Forgive my impatience, Lord,
Increase my trust in You.

While reflecting on my impatience, a different sound above me captured my attention. Gliding through the skies, cawing to me, was the raven again! I had not left all my friends behind!

I recorded the obvious lesson:

I see the raven daily—what a precious reminder of God's care. We moved places today—it was difficult for me, but again God's Word spoke. No matter where I go, He *is* with me—to the highest mountain or depths of the sea.

When I returned to camp several hours later, I found my cot had arrived by muleback with several other necessities, including a goatskin full of water and a bowl of porridge for the E.L.F. The old *adde* was still providing the meals for the E.L.F.; the umbilical cord to the village had not been severed. Why then had we left in the first place?

My cot hugged the west wall of the hut. Logs protruding from the side of the hut forced me to ease carefully in and out of bed. Four feet away lay Sayeed's ground cloth; his knapsack hung on a log. Berhane and another soldier slept outside to keep guard. Bekeet returned to his village.

The rest of the day would have been uneventful except for a small green insect I saw moving in the grass during a later walk. I sat on a rock and watched it for a long time; it almost resembled a clump of grass itself. Finally the insect positioned its lanky legs delicately onto a blade of grass that jutted out the side of a rock. Moments later it jumped over to my rock. No longer blending with the green grass, the insect's threadlike body looked naked and vulnerable as it glided carefully across the rock and headed back toward the grass.

Minutes passed before it reached the end of the rock. One foreleg then crossed stealthily over the narrow abyss separating the rock and a blade of green grass. Pulling the grass toward the rock, the insect cautiously placed another foreleg onto the blade and gradually pulled its entire body over. The insect had made it home!

My own precarious situation was like the insect's. I too was out of my natural environment. Under the scrutiny of armed men in the wilderness, I felt naked and vulnerable. I saw myself making the same desperate attempt to be home, to be at rest, to be myself. But my own strength was failing. My trust had to be in Someone much greater—greater than myself, greater than the men I was with, greater than the passion that impelled the men to imprison me, greater than the fear that often dominated me.

Would I make it home like the insect? I felt so alienated. I needed and wanted to trust that God would bridge that abyss and allow me to pass over to the green blade. But while I remained yet exposed and defenseless, I needed God's protection.

I was so impressed by the lesson God taught me that I entered in my notebook:

> I scarcely knew you were an insect
> Until your slender green body
> Jumped high off that blade of grass.
> How perfectly God protects you
> From your predators.
>
> So too does my God
> (Who created you also)
> Protect me from Satan's darts of
> Dejection, despair, discouragement, disease,
> And doubt—
> For the blood of Jesus covers me.

The days that followed blurred into each other. No word came from Adam. Boredom and restlessness gnawed at me. Fearful that time would become irrelevant and that my mind would lapse into confusion, I sought to keep myself occupied. One way would be to resume my embroidery. I had finished embroidering the Psalm on the triangular bandage, and with no space left to continue, I turned to the white veil. I also needed more embroidery thread and remembered the yard of striped material. Stripping apart three single threads from the crosswise grain, I rolled and twisted them together. Then with my pen I sketched the fourth verse of Psalm 34 onto the veil, bordering it with semblances of tiny mountain flowers I had seen:

O MAGNIFY THE LORD WITH ME
LET US EXALT HIS NAME TOGETHER.

"Together." I thought of the person with whom I really longed to magnify the Lord. Karl and I were not together. We were apart . . . far apart . . . perhaps forever. I looked at the men who kept me from Karl. As I did so, I wanted to lash out at them. What did they really want anyway? Why was I not hearing anything from the leaders? I addressed Sayeed, unable to restrain myself any longer:

"Sayeed, please, I will not last long in these mountains. I am beginning to feel sick in my stomach. I will get worms. My baby will not be well. I can't keep on. Please tell Adam."

"You will go when we hear from Adam. Maybe Monday," came his reply through Berhane.

"But if you want me to be released well, I must go now. I'm feeling sick," I persisted, taking advantage of the nausea that was starting to develop.

"O.K. I'll send someone to telephone Adam. I will tell him you are sick."

I wanted to believe him. I struggled with my senses, telling myself there had to be a telephone nearby. For a while I did believe him. I would not entertain any other thought. I had to have hope somehow.

But again I felt empty. Of course there could be no telephone in such a wilderness. Even if there were, Adam would not be near one. I hoped in nothing. My dreams were a delusion.

I went to a large rock to escape the surveillance of the men. I let the tears come. I had failed. The silly hope that being sick would release me was deceptive self-reliance. My hatred did not magnify the Lord. For a long time I poured out myself to God and then continued writing in my notebook:

> I am tempted so to beg from my enemies release
> But I know release is not theirs
> To give.
> It is Thine.
> Lord, release me first from my own fear.
> Reveal to me again my
> Freedom in You.

The days were as empty for my guards as they were for me. Their only excitement was the arrival of lunch and again supper, along with any village gossip that accompanied it. Occasionally they cleaned their rifle barrels and rehearsed military drills.

I was watching them clean their rifles one morning as I lay resting in the hut. All was quiet . . . except for the developing life inside me. At first I thought it was only gas pains or stomach cramps; then I held my breath and waited. Again a quiver, a twinge, a tickle in my abdomen. And then again, a little stronger. It was the first positive sign that our baby was well! Running outside, I found my rock and opened my heart in praise to God:

> This child within me—
> I feel him move!
> Evidence again of that *great*
> Gift of life You give.
> Oh, God, make me worthy
> To be his mother
> And grant him the joy
> Of *new* birth in You.

I sat savoring the moment for a time. It was our child, whom God had given, and He had spared our child's life. But Karl . . . he would not know about that moment. The child was conceived, nurtured, developed, and moved within *me*. Karl would not have that comfort of God that his child was well. I wanted to comfort Karl, to place his hand on my abdomen to feel the movements.

Because I could not write to Karl, I wrote my prayer to God:

Be with my beloved husband
This day, O Father;
In his loneliness
Comfort him
With the same love with which
You comfort me;
Deal with us tenderly
For we are needy sheep;
Lead us to that rich pasture land
Of service together
For Your glory.

A visitor came to the hut that morning. A nomadic shepherd from a nearby hill had heard that a pregnant woman was at the camp, and he brought a gift of warm frothy goat's milk. In the blackened mud-and-grass bowl several strands of hair and blades of grass floated on the milk. I could detect the fleshy odor of goats. My stomach protested. Though I was grateful for the milk and encouraged by the shepherd's thoughtfulness, it was difficult to drink. I did so only because the milk was nutritious and I had to keep up my strength.

I washed the milk down with tea because it was teatime anyway. I had a new tea glass, purchased at the same "store" as the sugar and tea. My first tea glass had disappeared in our move, and Sayeed ordered a new one. It was a flowered one, larger than any of the others. Since Eritreans considered it impolite to offer a glass of tea only half full, it meant that from then on I would be getting more tea than anyone else.

Sayeed, however, became interested in another drink. In the box of groceries there was a can of American instant coffee. Intrigued by the fact that the coffee beans were already roasted and ground and that only boiling water had to be added, he wanted to try it. Using a stick, he dumped three times as much coffee as needed into his glass—enough to choke any American—and added as much sugar. He filled his glass a third full with water, stirred it, and sipped it slowly. Enjoying it fully, he encouraged the others to try the *"boon cob America."* The spectacular drink came to have more appeal than the local beer.

We also had an unusual meal one night. Berhane had gone scouting in the afternoon and returned with the news that he had spotted a wild animal. Sayeed granted him permission to kill it. The sound of rifle shots pierced the valleys. I shuddered at the vivid recollection of Anna's falling to the ground. I would rather have opened another can of meat than to eat fresh meat that night.

Berhane returned to camp, hauling the bodies of two wiry-haired, short-legged animals. The men went to work skinning the animals and cutting up the meat. They portioned out some of the best parts of the animals for me to eat. I cooked mine separately, adding some catsup to disguise the taste. The meat, although somewhat stringy, tasted much like beef.

Following the meal, Sayeed prepared for prayer to Allah. His religion dictated that he remove his shoes and wash his feet and hands. When no water was available, he scraped his hands and feet ceremoniously in the dirt to "wash" them. Completing that part of the ritual, he stood erect and faced toward Mecca beyond.

My heart cried out for him:

> He cries to his god—
> Removes his shoes and faces toward
> The east.
> He says he is praying for me—
> But, O God, how it slanders Your Name,
> For his god is not there.
>
> But You are there—
> And You are *here,*
> And You have reminded me

That all may come to You,
Just as we are—sinful, repentant,
Unworthy—
And You answer.

And too, You remind me again
Of the many others in *Your* fellowship
Praying for me—
And You hear the fervent prayer of the
Faithful in *You.*

And Lord God—I give You praise
That Jesus Himself prayed for me
Before His death—
And even now is interceding.

Be pleased to answer,
According to Your masterful plan.

On Sunday, June 9, Sayeed awoke early as usual. In fact, he seldom slept well at night, and then only in fitful intervals. I felt like suggesting that if he did not sleep so much during the day, sleeping at night would come easier for all of us.

Mornings were often the hardest time of the day for me, although I felt most susceptible to bouts with depression later as the day dragged on endlessly. Usually by evening I could rationalize that another day was gone, and I was . . . perhaps . . . a bit closer to home. But each morning I had to face the fact that I was still a captive. The stiffened animal skins I lay on were not yet replaced with the spongy foam rubber mattress of home. My bed did not yet welcome Karl, and Karl's arms were not there to nestle into before reaching out to the world. I faced that Sunday morning bitterly, for it seemed no different from any other.

Sayeed, in his usual routine, reached first for his radio. I never saw him without it. It was his baby, and he handled it carefully. The day we moved he had wrapped the radio in a green cloth sack, made to fit snuggly around it, and carried it himself. I had the distinct impression he trusted no one else with it.

But most unexpectedly on that morning, nearly two weeks after my abduction, he entrusted the radio to me. At seven o'clock he had listened to what must have been very bland news on an Arabic station, broadcasting from Great Britain, and then he impulsively handed it over.

I accepted the radio gloomily, and halfheartedly toyed with the dial as I lay on my cot. I had not the slightest idea what any of the three bands meant. The babble of unfamiliar languages squealed through the box as I switched to another band and turned the dial back and forth. Nothing except a lot of static and high-pitched music. One more band, I thought, and then give up. Still the same. One more try—and I switched back to the first band.

My fingers stopped paralyzed on the dial. There it was—English! I raised the volume and pressed my ear closer. A man was giving a speech. No, not a speech—a sermon. I listened intently to the words:

"What do we do when problems come our way, when we are faced with separation from someone we love, when we come to the utter end of our own resources?"

I could not believe my ears. He was speaking directly to me.

". . . to be sure, life situations change. We may find ourselves cast down by insurmountable problems, feeling alienated even from ourselves. Everything about us may change . . . but there is one thing that is changeless. God's Word stands unmoved. God Himself cannot change. It is in Him we must put our confidence and find Him completely able to bring a solution . . . and peace."

Clutching the radio tightly in my hands, I held on to each word. He closed with Scripture, the first I had heard in two weeks:

" 'The Lord bless you, and keep you; the Lord make His face shine on you, and be gracious to you; the Lord lift up His countenance on you, and give you peace.' "

The voice faded. An announcer stated he hoped we would tune in again to Radio Voice of the Gospel, broadcasting from Addis Ababa the same time the next morning, and for twenty minutes in the evening. Then the English clipped off and a Swahili service began.

Still clutching the radio, I dropped my head and buried my tears in the sleeping bag. God's face had shone upon me. That shining remembrance of God's changeless nature and His special love never left me.

I handed the radio back and went outside for another kind of worship service. The gentle morning breeze became the organ music. The raven thundered applause in praise to the Creator as it flapped vigorously overhead, sweeping the majestic mountains. Flowers poked around rocks, splashed color lavishly over the dry brown earth, and shouted that God was everywhere. I too joined the song of praise and wrote another poem:

> You reminded me again
> That Your beauty is here—
> In that multicolored butterfly
> That just posed on the rock,
> In that white-tailed bird
> That so gracefully soared through the valley,
> In the excited cry of glee in a child
> Over there herding sheep.
> Thank You, God, for these reminders
> In this place where evil besets me.
> *You* are here.

The service continued all day, everywhere I went. Neither pews nor soft carpeting nor spreading arched rafters were required . . . only a humbled heart of praise to the God who was everywhere. I was changing. I was learning what it meant really to praise God and to know the joy exuding from such praise. As I meditated on God's love for me, I began to feel a new tenderness for the men holding me for ransom. I looked at Sayeed poking the fire—he was a lonely man without his family, seeking peace in a way that waged war. Berhane, too—he was eager and enthusiastic yet restless in a war that did not bring inner peace.

101

A portion of the *netsula* that Debbie embroidered in captivity. The verse is from Psalm 34:3.

For the first time I began to see them as people, not as men with rifles.

Early Thursday morning, June 6, Ramadan himself drove an army escort to Asmara with the letter; but the escort directed him to the army headquarters, not to us. Once there, Ramadan was told to leave, and a copy of the letter was finally forwarded to us at the consulate later in the morning. Jim, Ben, and I went to pick it up.

The single sheet of paper contained two letters; the first was from Debbie. Five days had passed since she wrote it. I read it slowly, lingering at each word. She was well! And she was trusting God! What strength that gave to me. I read on quickly. The second letter was from the Executive Committee.

	Notice	Date June 3/74
Eritrean Liberation Front		Executive Committee
To whom it may concern	American Evangelical Mission	

    The Executive Committee here sends a letter of quick contact about Mrs. Debra's case. And now we are sending you this letter requesting the following points (a) we are now asking you for quick contact again in two days, carrying the following things (b) clothes for her (c) oranges, fruit, any juice, cheese, canned ham, Dongollo [mineral] water, tuna fish, tomatoes, eggs, pasta eggs [spaghetti], soup, and teeth brush.

"A grocery list!" I exploded. I did not know whether to laugh or to cry. "Imagine the E.L.F. sending a 'quick contact' for groceries!" Did it mean that they were planning on a long stay for Debbie and wanted more food for the ensuing days? Ten days had passed already. The Tenneco Oil Company had sent several grocery boxes to their men, but still the men were not free. The letter at least reaffirmed Grant's words that Debbie was well and was treated with consideration. The E.L.F. had written the letter three days before. Their "quick contact" was a day overdue!

We examined the first E.L.F. letters again, checking for content and consistency. The letters said nothing! They failed to explain the reason either for the raid or for the demands. Debbie had written about medicines, stating that her quick release would depend upon a quick meeting of the demands. We did notice three important things about the letters. First was the enumeration on the paper. The first letter from Debbie to the American Consulate and the mission was numbered 0814. The first letter from the E.L.F. was 0815. The second letter we had just received was 0834. The handwriting on the E.L.F. letters matched. The seals imprinted on the letters were those of the Executive Committee. If nothing else, at least we knew the source of the letters was the same.

"There's not much we can write in reply to this," I commented after we had finished discussing the letter.

"No," Bob Perry said, "but you'd better write just to keep the lines of communication open. Send a letter or even two letters with the goods."

It seemed like sound advice, and I sat down to formulate another letter. I dated it June 6, 10:30 A.M.:

Dear Sirs, We have just received your letter dated June 3 (No. 0834). The only other letter we have received was dated May 29 (No. 0815). If you wrote any letter to us other than these, it *was not received*. Please inform your messengers to be careful to whom they deliver the letter. The one who gives you this letter is in direct contact with us and is authorized by us to carry your messages to us.

I repeat, please send all your messages by this messenger. We are very concerned about Mrs. Debbie's health and her needs. We will try to send the goods with this letter.

I signed the letter. It said nothing, but then there was nothing to say.

Jim suggested, "I think we should just give the letter to Ramadan and not bother with sending duplicates. He has friends that live out there, and they will be able to find where Debbie is. I say nuts on those shumes in Afabet. They don't seem to do anything."

True. We had hoped the Afabet shumes would help, but their help had been no better than Mohammed's words or Haile's promise.

I also want to tell Debbie what is going on, I thought to myself. It has been ten days since Debbie was taken. She must be wondering what is wrong. It will be nearly two weeks by the time this letter arrives. Perhaps I could write a short note to her very close to the end of my letter to the E.L.F. Perhaps they will let her read her note, and at the same time she will be able to read the letter to the E.L.F.

For the time I just sat and struggled to write. What could I say in a few short lines? How could I tell of my longing for her? How could I tell her how much I needed and missed her? How could I encourage her, rather than cause her more discouragement? How could I begin to tell her of the strength and encouragement that the Lord had given me? How could I share my joy that God was caring for her? I longed to send her a Bible so that she might read God's words of hope, and not have to rely on memory alone.

"Dear Deb," I wrote, and then groped for the words. "My love and prayers continue with you." Not just *for* her, I thought, but *with* her. She will understand . . . ours is a three-way relationship . . . she has been praying, now I have assured her that I am praying with her.

Debbie's greatest concern, I figured, would be my welfare. That was the way she was, so I continued: "I know of God's continued presence with you and praise Him." She will know, I thought, that God has given me a peaceful state of mind even as He has her.

I closed with a sentence to encourage her about the negotiations: "We pray that you may soon be with us." By God's might alone would she be released.

After writing the letter, I glanced at my watch. It was noon. I gulped. All the shops would close at one o'clock for siesta and would not reopen until three o'clock. Three o'clock was when the bus left for Ghinda. All the supplies had to be gathered in only one hour.

"C'mon, we've gotta get going," I nearly shouted.

The reason was apparent to everyone. The shops in Asmara were not exactly giant supermarkets. I would have to go to many tiny shops to buy the foodstuffs on the list: one place for fruit, another for canned goods, another for mineral water, another for dried fruit such as prunes and apricots, and yet another for cheese. Although Asmara was not large, it was not easy to get around in. Bicycles and careless pedestrians wandered indiscriminately on the streets and horse or donkey carts frequently blocked the path, to say nothing of the "I'm-already-late" car drivers honking their way into traffic jams.

Scurrying about the city, we completed the shopping list only minutes before siesta began. When we returned to the S.I.M. for lunch, another thought hit me. The army had received the letter before we did; they too knew what was on the shopping list! They would be expecting someone to leave Asmara with those goods. We did not want to incriminate anyone by sending him with the grocery items. We decided to leave the recently purchased items in Asmara and instead have Ramadan gather the things from our houses in Ghinda.

I wrote out a list for him that included clothes, soap, toothbrush, and food. At the top of the list was "Bible," the one item I knew Debbie had to have. She could survive on one dress, or on the local food, but without God's Word she would be hard-pressed to find His comfort and peace should the ordeal continue. Several small pocket Bibles were stacked in the chapel. Ramadan could get one of those.

When Ramadan returned from Ghinda the next morning, we learned that our preparations had accomplished nothing. Rather than go himself with the letter for the E.L.F., Ramadan had sent another messenger.

"One of my good friends has a brother who owns land in Sheib," he told us. Sheib was an area close to where we thought Debbie was. "He knows the land well," Ramadan continued, "and will take the letter, but he didn't want to take the goods. There were too many!"

I groaned. A letter would go, saying, "Here are the goods," and no goods would be there. The letter would be carried by an official courier . . . afraid to handle the goods. The Afabet shumes were now our only hope, but Monday was the soonest we could even get supplies to Afabet. The round trip by bus for a mission worker to come from Afabet for the goods and return would take four days. Getting supplies to Debbie quickly seemed impossible. I could not believe that we had been foiled—especially in sending her a Bible. I sank into my bed that night, realizing that again I had put hope and confidence in what men could do. Their promises had failed every time, yet I still looked to them for the solution.

I awoke Saturday morning, June 8, with one thought resounding in my mind: *wait.* It would be several days before the Ghinda messenger returned. The necessary items would not reach Debbie for many days. Until some message was returned I could only wait. As a college student I had learned about waiting. I recalled the passage from the Book of Ruth. Ruth had done all she could to have her relative Boaz redeem the land and inheritance of her deceased husband. Naomi, her mother-in-law, gave the sound advice to "sit still . . . until thou know how the matter will fall" (KJV).

I could distinctly remember the first time I had encountered that portion of Scripture. It was my first year at Wheaton, and I worked three times a week doing odd jobs for the maintenance department. One day I was assigned to dust the Student Union building. That afternoon a rather elderly (I thought) janitor came up to me and said he wanted to show me something. Taking me into a broom and supply closet, he shut the door, and I wondered what kind of dusting secret he was going to bequeathe to me. Instead of pulling dusting spray out of a box, he took a booklet off the shelf. He pressed it into my hand.

"I don't know how to talk very well," he had said a bit shakily, "but I saw you working and wanted to share this with you. It has taught me a lot about trusting God for His time schedule in the events of my life."

He had asked if we could pray—which we did—and then sent me back to my feather-flopping business, leaving me to wonder about the janitor who cleaned a spiritual house. Later I read the booklet, which looked like a dusty, boring, shirt-collar-grabbing tract. Instead of all that, it changed my thinking radically. I was at a point of telling God what was good for my life—that there was a certain young lady that fit my description of an ideal life partner. It was one of those indescribable feelings that almost every man has sometime in life when he finds the woman who sets his heart ticking like none other. She kept my eyes busy looking at her, and yet, to put it plainly, she could not stand me. If only the Lord would listen to me. I had it all worked out.

But the booklet with words of Scripture had told me to sit *still* until I knew how the matter would turn out. In other words, I was to wait for God's time. When finally I learned the lesson and asked the Lord to teach me to sit with peace in my heart for His provision of a wife—well, I ended up marrying her three years later.

I got out of bed at the S.I.M. and went to breakfast—rubbery oatmeal and cold burned toast that we always had. I thought about those words of Scripture, "Sit still." It was a command, not something optional. It meant to be still and calm in heart, in my emotions, even as I awaited meaningful contact about Debbie. Little things like getting a box of supplies to Debbie were to be in God's time schedule.

The daily radio calls to outlying mission stations were not supposed to be interesting that morning, but I went to listen anyway. First, the S.I.M. headquarters in Addis Ababa called all their stations. Then Asmara headquarters called all their stations. Afabet was nearly the last station to be called, and the standard question was put out:

"Do you have any traffic for us? Over."

"We have news," came the static-splintered reply. "Repeat. We have news for you. Please have Martin fly here tomorrow. Repeat. Can Martin fly here tomorrow? Over."

My heart did a double-take.

"Is it good news? Over," went the reply.

"Yes, it is important for a plane to come tomorrow. Over." Afabet was making it clear that Martin Katschall was wanted there for a meeting. We had a standing agreement that a plane would go if, and only if, the shumes in Afabet were planning to send Debbie out. But the ensuing questions and answers indicated that no "equipment" was then in Afabet. Debbie probably would not be on the plane, but then again she might be.

Finding a plane and a pilot was not going to be easy. The citizens' radio had announced the shooting of a German motorist who had been warned by the E.L.F. not to drive on the road. Several buses had been blown up by the E.L.F., and a telephone station was reduced to a gravel pit. That few pilots cared to fly north toward the E.L.F. stronghold was therefore not surprising. We finally convinced one to go, but he would not stay for the meeting; rather he would go back in the afternoon to pick up Martin when it was all over.

Sunday, June 9, I took Martin out to the airport about eight-thirty before church or Sunday school had begun. We prayed before he left, and I found it difficult to contain my excitement. The hope of seeing Debbie, maybe even that day, welled within me. She seemed near, yet so far away. The fulfillment seemed imminent, and it intensified my longing to have her with me again. Once more I waited.

Scarcely had the afternoon begun when Abo Meskel, a shop-keeper in Ghinda, came to the S.I.M. in Asmara. He was dressed in a business suit and always had a rather stately and proud air like an American southern aristocrat of a century earlier. When he knocked on my door he was clearly disturbed, although none of his stateliness was gone. I invited him into my room. He immediately closed the door tightly and began to explain himself in broken English, never having studied the language. Whenever we met, he would seldom speak except through an interpreter.

"In my house, this morning, they came early. Maybe eight. They knock on door. They give me this."

His extended hand held a tightly folded, familiar-looking paper. Obviously it had been hidden in his clothing. He continued to speak, his voice straining with emotion and force:

"They say if I give to someone not you, they kill me."

I unfolded the crumpled paper. The letter contained not one, but two pieces of paper, dated 6/9/74. It was written only that morning, probably in Ghinda. Abo Meskel's quivering voice heightened my anxiety. My heart throbbed. My hands shook.

The Eritrean Liberation Front.
Executive Committee.

To American Evangelical Mission Ghinda Hospital

The executive committee sends three letters to those whom they concern Mrs. Debra [Debbie] case. In our previous letters the committee were advising the mission for quick contact. And now because we do not get any reply, we are also persuaded ourselves to write this letter and we like to indicate the following instructions through this instructions the mission could direct contact the committee and try to fulfill it. The points are the following:

a. Send any person in Mario plantation in Hara in Date 6/10/74 at 9 o'clock in the morning.

b. The person who come to this place please send with him food, clothes and some medicines like (malaria pills and vitamins) for Mrs. Debra.

c. You may send a messenger or you may come yourselves for contact.

Notice

DO NOT miss the appointment. It is in the Mario plantation in Tigrinya.

The E.L.F. Executive Committee

Wow! It was the most daring, most direct, and most necessary letter we could hope for. It was no wonder Abo Meskel had been threatened with his life. Had that letter fallen into the hands of the army, it would booby-trap the leaders that held Debbie. The directness of the letter gave hope. Debbie was certain to get the clothes and food. But the directness was also limiting. I could not personally meet with the E.L.F. leaders. I spoke no Tigrinya, and even if I could go with a translator, my white face would alert everyone to the location and importance of the meeting. But despite the known danger, something inside kept needling me to meet personally in the oasislike plantation. Nevertheless, I could not go, for the army would not let a foreigner off the road.

When I asked Abo Meskel if he would carry a message back to Ghinda for me, dismay filled his voice.

"No! No! I stay here. Tomorrow I go to Ghinda."

Tomorrow would be too late. The plantation meeting was to be the next morning at nine. The bus would not even arrive at Ghinda until eight. In fact, when I thought about it, I had never even heard of the plantation, nor did I know where it was. Checking with Jim yielded a blank stare. Only a very old and abandoned plantation in the Ghinda area could be so completely unknown to us. Certainly if we did not know where to go, we could not very well get there.

Location immediately posed other problems. How far a messenger would have to walk and when he would have to leave were dependent upon where the place was. But who would go? It had to be someone reliable who knew the details to date. Only one person fit that description: Saleh. He knew the terrain, was physically fit, made friends easily, and spoke Arabic and Tigre well. His first language was Tigrinya, but in order to find directions and "make friends" he would need both the Tigre and Arabic languages. Most important was that he had said he was willing to do anything.

Jim left the S.I.M. compound with Abo Meskel, and they parted outside. Jim then went off to find someone who might have an old Italian map with the old roads, paths, and plantations on it. Abo Meskel disappeared. Probably he did not want to be seen or thought about any more. To his great relief he had completed his errand.

111

A detailed map of Eritrea was difficult to find, but a detailed old map was next to impossible. Fortunately, Jim found an old Italian who knew the wilderness areas and the Mario plantation. The man had an old map, and although it did not show the actual farming area, he was able to pinpoint it. The man had hunted there many times years before and described the hills, riverbeds, and rocks that would guide us.

With that information we calculated the time required to go from Ghinda and return. Most of the afternoon was used to assemble all the details. We then had to relay the message by telephone to Saleh, who was willing to go to the plantation and was waiting in Ghinda. We would have to be cautious, for although we had a telephone in the hospital, the message still would not be easy to transmit. All the Ghinda operators knew what had happened and listened eagerly for additional news. In order to avoid alerting all of Ghinda and the army as to the rendezvous location, several telephone calls to Saleh were made at thirty-minute intervals, each time giving only a part of the essential information.

Martin Katschall was due back from Afabet at six o'clock. When I arrived at the airport, the plane had not yet landed. Unlike my previous wait at the airport when Birchal had returned, I knew Debbie would not be on the plane; the letter telling us to meet at the plantation convinced me Debbie was still a captive. I was keen to hear, however, what Martin had learned and why the shumes had insisted he fly to Afabet. I wondered if the shumes would confirm what already seemed definite in my mind: that Debbie really was in the Afabet area and had never been moved. There was no other explanation for the last E.L.F. letter. It had been written and sent from Ghinda, yet Ghinda was east of Asmara and Debbie reportedly was west of Asmara.

I must have been looking anxious, for when Martin finally arrived his first words were, "Sorry, I wish I could have brought her to you."

"I didn't expect you to," I replied. "We've had more news."

Back at the S.I.M. Jim, Ben, and I sat down while Martin

unloaded his information. The only purpose of the meeting was to extend an apology.

"Just an apology?" I questioned in unbelief.

"Yes," he replied somewhat irked. "The shumes wanted to apologize, since they had obviously erred and did not want to appear deceitful. They stated that their earlier information about Debbie's movements had not been checked out."

All the donkey changes and dry riverbed trails to an unknown point southwest of Afabet were true, but they had nothing to do with Debbie, for she was not included. Since the shumes had been wrong, they apologized repeatedly. "From now on," they had told Martin, "we will tell you only those things that we have seen with our own eyes and heard with our own ears."

They next had told him that the three respected sheikhs had gone to the village where Debbie was held and had asked for her release.

Ben Motis knew the three sheikhs and was amazed that they had gone personally, for their influence was so great that an emissary was usually entrusted to accomplish any task. One of the sheikhs was thought to be a relative of *the* Mohammed, the self-proclaimed prophet of Allah. As a distant relative the Afabet sheikh himself was nearly worshiped. I was aware of the built-in structure and power of the Muslim society that inhabited the countryside: lowest were the shumes (elders) and highest, the sheikhs (religious leaders). I was speechless when Martin relayed what had happened as those sheikhs reached the E.L.F. band that held Debbie.

"The leaders are hard men," the sheikhs had disclosed. "We were circled when we got there and told we would have no discussion about Mrs. Debbie. We were allowed to walk in freedom back to our villages, but if we stayed, we would be carried out with bullets in our backs."

Strong words had been delivered to strong men. The sheikhs realized for the first time that the E.L.F. were not readily influenced by their demands. The discovery that the E.L.F. seemed not to be a movement controlled by the people but one ruling the people was shocking to the sheikhs—and to us. We had been sure the Lord would use the authority and position of the sheikhs to effect Debbie's release.

Sunday night was quiet like most of my other Sundays. In the quiet I thought. A clear picture emerged. Beginning at the first prayer session after the kidnapping, I had prayed that God's hand alone would deliver Debbie. That prayer was being answered. Mohammed's words of promise to us had been unfulfilled. Haile apparently had never forwarded our reply letter. The Afabet shumes had given inaccurate information. The first messenger had failed to carry in the supplies. The powerful sheikhs had proved impotent. What was left?

I sat down to write my parents for the first time since Debbie had been taken. A mail strike, just resolved, had prevented my writing earlier.

> . . . In any event prayer must continue. From man's point of view the situation is hopeless and becoming more so each day. This, of course, only means a greater opportunity to see the hand of God demonstrated.
>
> God's people throughout the world are praying. Anna is singing praises at our King's feet and so ought we. These things have brought us all closer to Him in fellowship at His feet.
>
> In His perfect time the situation will be resolved. Still, in all, it is difficult to sit still. . . .

All day Monday I waited and wondered what might be happening at the Mario plantation. Monday night I decided to join the "apartment crew," as I had come to call them. The Steltzers, Greet, and Sandra, the four who stayed in the mission apartment, would gather each evening to sing, read Scripture, and pray. I realized that I had not spent much time with them since I was in Asmara. All my activities had focused where Jim and I stayed at the S.I.M. on the other side of town. That night, in the time of painful waiting, I needed the activity of praise and prayer.

Tuesday morning brought no word from Ghinda. The afternoon

crept by. Still no word. In the evening I again went to the apartment. I telephoned the hospital, but they had heard nothing of Saleh, nor had they seen him.

Wednesday, June 12, began without Saleh's having surfaced. About eleven o'clock in the morning Jim called the hospital to ask one of the workers to go to Saleh's house—perhaps someone there would have heard. A half hour later Saleh called us; he had been sleeping. There was no rush, for another rendezvous had been scheduled for Friday. That afternoon, Saleh said, he would be in Asmara.

At one o'clock Saleh brought another letter.

An Ethiopian Orthodox "Keshie" or priest poses with his cross. The priests commonly wear beards and always carry a hand-held cross for devotees to kiss. *Greet Rietkerk*

CHAPTER 5

The Sunday evening was cool as usual, and I pulled the striped material tighter around my shoulders and draped the towel over my knees as I sat near the fire. The men never built a roaring campfire that might attract attention, merely a soft glow of embers. There was little time to enjoy the warmth of the embers and the enticing dream world inside a flickering flame; the embers were crushed and blanketed soon after evening tea, the safety of darkness enveloping the camp.

The air grew too cold to stay outside, and I sought the warmth of my sleeping bag. Snuggling in, I did what I felt the most like doing just then: sing.

"He's got the whole world in His hands. . . ."

I stopped at the third verse, "He's got the tiny little baby in His hands. . . ." I thought about it a moment, and then sang out lustily. It was so true! God cared about and controlled the life of our tiny baby whom I did not even know yet.

Berhane entered the hut, and to my amazement asked me to teach him the song I was singing. He joined in enthusiastically after the second verse. We added a verse, "He's got the E.L.F. in His hands," and Berhane clapped in rhythm as we sang together.

Sayeed also came in and listened as the songfest continued.

"You see, Mrs. Debbie, we want you to be happy with us. When you sing, it makes us happy!" Berhane exclaimed.

"I'm not happy because I am a prisoner, Berhane," I replied. "I'm happy because Jesus does have me and the whole world in His hands, and it is His peace that makes me content."

"We're fighting for peace and contentment," Sayeed said with Berhane interpreting. "When the E.L.F. win our freedom, Eritreans will have peace and much more: education, health care, and productive farming. Then there will be freedom at its best."

"Those things are necessary, Sayeed," I said, "but freedom is not what you have. It's what you are. Jesus was a freedom fighter, and only He can make you content because He makes you right with God."

After more discussion I was surprised when Berhane interjected: "Mrs. Debbie, I would like to have a Bible. I want to learn more. Sayeed says he wants one too."

Before going to bed that night I borrowed a flashlight from Sayeed and wrote in my notebook: "June 9—Two men asked for Bibles today. Praise God! That is why He did not release me today."

It was to be the last meaningful communication with Berhane. The next morning he left hurriedly without saying good-by, and I never saw him again. It was then I realized I had lost a friend, not an enemy.

I wondered how I would be able to share anything with Sayeed. Apart from blundering through several Tigrinya greetings and the Arabic words for "Thank you" and "You're welcome," there was little else I could say. Communication challenged imagination. Sayeed had prided himself in being able to say "Thank you" in English, and he often sat down dutifully with a notebook and the English alphabet, grappling with the pronunciation. He had told me that after I was released I could send him an English Bible, for by then he would be able to read it!

My concern in not being able to communicate without Berhane was relieved that afternoon by an unusually young-looking man. When he reached our camp, he came inside the hut where I was sitting on the cot to shelter myself from the sun. He introduced himself. His English, although poor, was adequate for basic under-standing. He told me he had come to stay for a time. He was a member of Sayeed's platoon and had been summoned.

Osman was short and thin but somehow muscular. He chewed on a wad of tobacco and spat on the ground next to my feet as he talked about himself. I learned that he had been a disgruntled student. Unable to find a job or to advance himself, he had decided to join the E.L.F. after two years of listlessness.

Following our introduction, I gathered sticks to prepare a fire. The thought had struck me several days earlier that I was terribly selfish with my time and very self-centered in my actions. I had talked to war enthusiasts about the peace of Jesus without showing them the love of Jesus. Determined to change, I began to venture out of the shaded hut and into the blistering sun to prepare tea for the soldiers, the water carriers, and any new "visitors" to our camp.

While fanning the fire I pumped Osman to answer the questions burning in my mind: Had he come from Adam? Had he any word of my release? Had anyone seen Karl? When would I leave?

Osman's answer was simple. He was merely a soldier. Only the "masters" knew the answers. He never gave answers; he simply obeyed commands.

Two weeks, and still no word. I sought refuge again at my rock and sat for a long time watching a herd of goats scatter over the cliffs. The clink of their hoofs resounded through the valleys as they made their way across the brow of the mountain. I visualized the age-old Psalm of the Shepherd caring for his flock. Likening myself to David, the author of the Psalms who had lived in similar mountains, I paraphrased David's song:

The Lord is my Shepherd, I shall not want. (What greater provider and protector could I have?)

He makes me lie down in green pastures; He leads me beside the quiet waters. (Oh, God, all around are *stormy* waters—but You give me to drink from cool, quiet streams.)

He restores my soul; (Here in Your presence You restore me completely with Your Word, which stands forever.)

He guides me in the paths of righteousness for His name's sake. (Though Satan would so strongly tempt and disillusion, and my enemies would discourage—yet You, God, direct my steps, swift as hind's feet, because You love me and have not yet completed Your plan for me.)

Even though I walk through the valley of the shadow of death, I fear no evil; for Thou art with me; (Amen! I have been there and how precious was the reality of Your presence and strength—You delivered me from all my fears.)

Thy rod and Thy staff, they comfort me. (You provided me with a staff—to secure my faltering steps—how real is Your strength and now You keep me from harm and sickness and despair, as Your staff comforts.)

Thou dost prepare a table before me in the presence of my enemies; (Even ham for Sunday! You give the strength to eat, Lord, even when my heart would want to break. You are strengthening me and the little one within me for our safe return to our beloved one—Karl.)

Thou hast anointed my head with oil; (You have anointed me king and priest through Christ—because of His Kingship and Priesthood, You grant me access to You. You have made me to be a king and priest. What need do I have to fear the leaders of this world? What power have they? *All* power is Yours! And I am Yours, and the same power that raised Christ from the dead to be king and priest of all is within me! At Thy feet, oh, Jesus, all earthly leaders tremble. But I can rejoice, for You have anointed my head . . . You chose me before the foundations of the world. What marvelous mercy and love!)

My cup overflows. (You fill my tea glass so full! A reminder of Your great provision. Oh, I am filled with thanksgiving to You, and when my heart is heavy, and I come to You unfilled, how You satisfy my thirst, even in this dry land. Only You could do that, Lord.)

Surely goodness and lovingkindness will follow me all the days of my life, (Oh, God, my life is not yet over—You saved me from death when it was so near. You are yet preserving me when danger creeps all around in this perilous land. I can trust You surely to fulfill that work in me which You have begun—to use me to praise You before men—to uplift You so that You draw all men to Yourself—to be united in Your ministry—the ministry of the gospel with my life's partner whom You have given. I can't wait to share all these lessons You are teaching me with him! But God, help me to trust *You* for what is good for me.)

And I will dwell in the house of the Lord forever. (In Your time, God—what precious, everlasting hope!)

Amen!

Praise God!

Thoughts of Karl never left my mind. It was Tuesday, June 11, and I had been in the mountains away from him for sixteen days. It seemed like sixteen years. As I made tea that morning, I thought of my kitchen in Ghinda. Baking was a favorite hobby; Karl always enjoyed the fringe benefits. Homemade bread was his weekly request, and while I never looked forward to heavy kneading in 104-degree temperatures with perspiration rolling down my face, his never-failing exclamation of "You're the best bread baker in the whole world!" was well worth the effort. Perspiration was rolling down my face that morning, but I knew there would be no tender response from Karl for the tea I was making.

In Ghinda my life with Karl had been busy. Responsibilities were great. But whenever I was not on hospital call, Karl and I always took advantage of the chance to be together at mealtime. We enjoyed it leisurely, often by candlelight at supper. It was the time to enlighten each other on our respective activities, to discuss mission problems, hospital staff problems, to analyze a sermon or Bible study Karl had conducted, or to make a tape recording to send home. Our discussion around the table could easily be lengthened to fill most of the evening. Our marriage deepened there.

Mealtime since I had become a captive was different. I had no appetite to eat, although I could force myself. It was not the food I missed . . . it was Karl. I again sought God and shared what my heart was crying:

> I give praise to You for Karl
> For his faithful and constant
> Ever-deepening love—
> Founded on the One who loved us first.
> I give You praise for his authority
> And leadership in our home,
> Guided directly by Your hand.
> I give You praise for his teaching,
> For the direction he has given me
> Into the deeper truths of Your Word.
> I give You praise that his life
> Is hid in Your tender care.
> I praise You that You have granted
> To me that unmatched joy of
> Expressing Your love to him—
> Oh, Father, direct me back to him.

My thoughts continued to center on Karl as the day wore on.

I went to sleep peacefully that night but was awakened when I heard Sayeed tossing fitfully. I was always quick to hear any disturbance—I knew I had to be easily alerted to any impending danger. Sayeed was probably awake at that hour—it was three o'clock— because he had slept most of the day.

An insatiable thirst overpowered me. I seldom drank enough fluids during the day, since milk did not come regularly and tea was not made often. I had tried only once to purify the water by boiling because the single stained pot used for cooking gave the water a horrible rusty taste. In addition, boiled water took a long time to cool, and the pot was always in demand for other cooking.

I did, however, still have several cans of juices, and my hand moved along the ground until it lighted upon a can. It was unopened, and I was so thoroughly parched that I ventured to ask Sayeed to open it for me, despite the hour. He rose from his mat, and taking out his penknife, the only can opener we had, he punched two tiny slits in the top. I thanked him and sipped as much as I dared because I had to ration my supplies. Who knew how long they would have to last? I remembered Berhane's words of several days before. He had warned me to be careful with my food because I would get no more. At times I had felt tempted to devour it all in one large meal and thereby force my release. I had finally concluded, however, I would be hurting only myself.

Several minutes later Sayeed was still standing over me; he had not returned to his mat since he opened the can. I felt uncomfortable at his lingering, but attempted to ignore it and settled into my sleeping bag.

Suddenly a rough rigid hand touched my face, startling me. His curled fingers slid over my nose and lips, then over my chin and neck, and subtly swept over the top of my uniform . . . My heart stopped. He lifted his arm slowly, folded it into his other arm, and rested it on his chest. He stood there gazing at me for several long minutes before returning to his mat.

Unable to move, I lay frigid the rest of the night. What did Sayeed want? What did his touch mean? I wanted to think he was showing tender concern for me as a helpless kidnapped victim. Was it meant to be a soothing touch, as a father would give a child to console him in the midst of a nightmare? Or did his touch indicate something far more, something less innocent? For hours I lay awake, bracing myself silently for it to happen again. The last time I checked my watch, the luminous dial read five o'clock.

Daytime was usually less eventful. I met each morning with a prayer that God would help me to accept it, to live it, and to trust Him for *that* day. I could take only one day at a time. To anticipate perhaps hundreds of days with my captors would have been crushing.

I continued my embroidery. All the water carriers also had become interested and had willingly set to work stripping and twisting threads to make the embroidery floss. I had finished the fourth verse of Psalm 34 bordered with the mountain flowers. Next I started on Psalm 121, reminded of the sustaining strength at Anna's death.

At the same time I started another project: a treasure hunt to find varieties of wild flowers scattered on the plateau. The closer I scanned the area, the more species I found in different shapes and colors, shadowed beneath a thornbush, or blasted by the sun in the open earth, or sprouting in the crack of a rock. I sketched them on the inside front cover of my notebook, recording their peculiarities. I intended to find out their names after my release. I paused once more to reflect my feelings on paper:

> Oh, God, You are a God of detail—
> I see it in these mountain flowers,
> So minute, so unnoticed beneath
> The shadow of the rocks,
> Yet perfect in shape
> So full of variety in designs and colors—
> Many different expressions of Thy grace.
>
> So teach me, Lord,
> You have every detail worked out
> For my life.
> How can I then worry?
> You care infinitely about little things.

While the days had settled into a routine, the nights held more interruptions. Thursday night, June 13, my body did not seem tired, and I fought to drift off to sleep. The day had not been strenuous, and I remembered all too well what had happened the other night. My fear of a hyena attacking at night seemed insignificant as I looked at the man asleep across the hut. He always removed his pistol from its halter at night, laid it next to him, and covered it with a light cloth. I waited to hear his slow rhythmic breathing before I thought of sleeping myself. The night was a bit warmer and a sleeping bag was too hot, but I zipped myself inside it anyway for any protection it could afford from curious eyes or carelessly placed hands. I slept stiffly to avoid arousing attention by crackling the taut skins or creaking the unsteady cot legs beneath me.

Some time later I sensed a strange unsettling in the hut. The moon was gone, hidden beyond the other side of the hut, but lifting my eyes, I saw a dim outline standing over my bed. Sayeed! My knees quivered and his dark silhouette blurred in front of me as I sought to collect my thoughts, to keep a cool head. I tried to concentrate on a regular pattern of breathing, and on keeping my eyes closed in a natural manner of sleep. My heart thumped through my chest wall and pounded in my ears. I was afraid.

I prayed and I prayed. I reminded God of the promises in His Word to protect His own. I thanked Him for the protection already powerfully demonstrated in my life. I cried to Him to protect me from Sayeed. I remembered how long it had been since he had seen his wife . . . several years. I thought of how easy it would be for him to take advantage of the darkness and silence of the hut and of his brazen governorship over me while holding me in subjection with his weapon. But my life was Karl's—I was his and only his, and I violently feared a transgression of that.

God heard, and He answered. Scripture verses flooded my mind and brought a resurgence of comfort and peace.

Sayeed stood over me for what seemed an incomprehensible length of time before I heard his sandaled feet shuffle to the entrance of the hut as he left. I pulled the sleeping bag tighter about my chin and turned my stiffened body to face the wall. Minutes later he returned to the hut and finally settled onto his mat. I prayed vigilantly the rest of the night.

I welcomed the next morning more than any other since my captivity. I went to the rock. I had much to share with God, much praise to give Him, and many more fears to confide in Him.

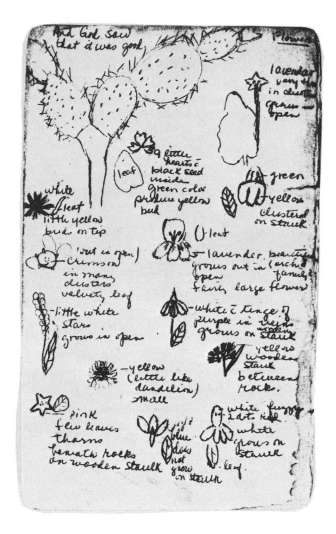

Pages from Debbie's notebook. At the left are sketches of wildflowers she saw in the mountains. At the right are some of the hymns and Scripture verses she recited frequently while being held captive.

Hidden in the hollow of His precious hand
Never foe can follow never traitor stand
We must trust Him wholly - all for us to do.
They who trust Him fully, find Him fully true
Stayed upon Jehovah - hearts are fully blessed
Finding as He promised perfect peace &
rest.

The Lord bless thee & keep thee
The Lord lift his countenance upon thee
And give thee peace
The Lord make his face to shine upon thee
And be gracious unto thee.
                    Num. 22.

Be of good cheer - I have overcome the
world. John 15?
nothing can separate us from love of God.
If my people which are called by my name -
Shall humble themselves & pray - then
will I answer from heaven ..."
I will satisfy them from the fat of the land.

Tried as by fire refined as gold they shall mount up like
wings of Eagle - they shall walk & not be
weary, they shall run & not faint
                              Is. ?
And the peace of God shall guard your
minds & hearts in Christ Jesus.
Come unto me all ye that are heavy laden
And I will give you rest.
Take my yoke upon your learn of me
for my yoke is easy & my burden is light.
Without a vision the people perish
Be of good cheer - I have overcome the world
Is there anything too hard for thy God?

Thou wilt keep him in perfect peace
whose mind is stayed on thee.

The fifth letter brought by Saleh from the E.L.F. on Wednesday, June 12, was handed to me in my room at the S.I.M. Saleh explained why he had not come immediately with it.

"I'm sorry, Mr. Karl"—he insisted on calling me that even though we were the same age—"but I was too tired. It was not three hours to get to the plantation, no, no, it took me *six* hours to go. I came there at eleven Monday, so I was not on time. When I found the men, they were very kind to me. Oooh! They fix me tea, they put their arms around me and call me brother. It was too hot, and they wanted me to rest, so we did not talk until afternoon."

"Did you have any difficulty with the supplies?" I asked, anxious that they reach Debbie soon.

"Oh, no, I dressed like a country man and tied all of the things around my chest and waist"—his gestures showed the articles had hung like link-sausage. Over the supplies Saleh wore a large flowing piece of material. Finally he told me, "They say Mrs. Debbie will get them in a day."

"Did you remember to get a Bible?" I wanted to hear Saleh's reassuring answer. Instead, silence. Hiding his face in his hands, Saleh shook his head.

"Oh, Mr. Karl, I forgot! I'm sorry! You see, I go to the house for some things. I go to the hospital for medicines. I go to my house to get ready. But I forgot to go to the chapel for the Bible."

A wave of nausea came over me. Debbie would not receive the one thing she needed the most. Saleh continued to describe his trip, but I only half-listened. Debbie . . . no Bible . . . would she understand?

"I told them you did not get the letters because of Haile," Saleh was saying, "and the army got one. The E.L.F. knew; that is why they send a letter making the appointment in the plantation. They say Mrs. Debbie is good; she is eating everything that the people eat, so they like her. She is happy and plays with the women and children that live there. Two men are the leaders, one is Adam. The other one, too, he is Yakob. He has a big bushy beard like you. They said they have not received any of your letters."

Saleh also had told them that we would not meet any demands until Debbie was released, but they said nothing. After talking for a long while, they prepared food for him to eat and also told him to spend the night there because of the long journey. In the morning he was given a letter to bring back, but its contents were not revealed. He left to return to Ghinda on Tuesday morning but had not actually arrived until early in the evening. The long rugged walk and his night on the desert had been exhausting.

"I slept on a mat. They were kind to me. But in the night big, *big* black ants eat me, and look—I have big bumps." He showed me all of his physical trophies from a night in the open desert. I was glad I had not gone. The graphic evidence convinced me easily that his excessive sleeping early Tuesday night and late that morning had been necessary.

The three-page letter lay before me; the pages were numbered 0859, 0860, 0861. The enumeration showed the paper was from the same tablet as the earlier letters. As I sat to read the letter, Ben and Jim joined me.

Eritrean Liberation Front
   Executive Committee   Date 6. 10. 74
      Announcement.

On May 27, 1974, an E.L.F. guerrilla unit entered to Ghinda American Evangelical Mission Hospital and took away (kidnapped) two nurses of the hospital, Mrs. Anna Strikwerda (dead) and Mrs. Debra (alive). After kidnapping events finished, we wrote four letters to the mission and acknowledged it all the things, after that one from your men comes and because of this, this letter directly arrives to you by this man. We are going to show you the instructions and requests for release of Mrs. Debra.

The requests and instructions are as follows:

A. Bring $5,000 (five thousands dollars)
    price of cholera medicines.
B. $5,000 (Five thousand dollars)
    malaria medicines.

I gulped hard; already that was ten thousand dollars that they demanded, and more was to follow . . .

C. Five (5) Tigrinya typewriters and two (2) English
    typewriters.
D. Two (2) Duplicators.
E. Seven (7) Battery microphones.

I had to laugh, even though it was no laughing matter. Imagine seeing seven typewriters, duplicators, and microphones swaying to and fro on a camel's back as it plodded into the desert! One would have thought that the E.L.F. had rented a suite in the World Trade Center rather than shuffling from one nomadic desert camp to another. But there was more . . .

F. $75,000 (Seventy-five thousands dollars).

Preposterous! Such demands would have to be rejected completely. We could not begin to meet them even if we were to sell the entire hospital. Still more . . .

G. The mission should have to announce in the Radio by the
    name of E.L.F. the following:
    (1) the E.L.F. feels a lot of sorrow and great grief by (about)
        the death of Mrs. Anna Strikwerda.
    (2) from Date 3. 27. 74 til now cholera disease spreads in
        Eritrea and until now there are 352 (three hundred
        fifty-two) persons dead in the villages. The disease is going
        on (spreading) terribly. Therefore the E.L.F. asks aid from
        all over the world those who cares for Eritrean people
        specially.
    (3) If the mission fulfills all the requests given to her by E.L.F.
        we are going to release Mrs. Debra after ten hours.

It was no surprise that they wanted radio announcements. They were eager for all the publicity they could get. I had no doubt that they were sorry about Anna's death, for it had caused them great trouble and bad publicity, but if they were really sorry, they could have released Debbie many days earlier. Finally I came to the last of the long and impossible letter.

Notice

Mrs. Deborah (Debbie) is now in a good physical and mental condition. She is in the camps somewhere in the liberated areas. And her case is different from the case of the five Tenneco personalities it has not any relation. . . . And all these things is now —American mission affair, therefore, don't try to relate the cases of Mrs. Debra with that case. As we say before, we are going to release her as soon as the requests finishes.

Eritrean Liberation Front
Executive Committee

I hesitated over the significance of the "Notice." Fortunately for us, the E.L.F. seemed to recognize Saleh as "official." More than ever I realized how difficult it was to be "different from" Tenneco. We certainly wanted it that way, the E.L.F. said they wanted it that way, but obviously the E.L.F. were confused. For them to think that our small shoestring-budgeted mission could pay over $85,000 was clear evidence that they considered missionaries to be oil barons. It was also obvious that Saleh's words had not been heeded. He had told them that no ransom would be paid.

I understood what had happened, though; it was simple bargaining. If, for example, I were to enter an Ethiopian shoe shop to ask the price of a pair of shoes, I might be quoted a price of $15— outlandishly high, but then I was a rich foreigner (so they would think). I would throw up my hands in pretended disgust and shout, "What? I would not pay five dollars for those!" But the shopkeeper knew I would, and I knew he would not charge fifteen dollars. Eventually I would buy the shoes for $10. With the E.L.F. I had said "Nothing" was my offer. They in good barter had said $85,000 plus. Apparently the E.L.F. thought that the mission was bargaining and really would pay money; they therefore went ahead and made demands.

The painful truth was that we were not bargaining, we were not playing games, and the stakes were high. I knew that according to our mission policy, no ransom could be paid. But I also knew that money had been paid when the E.L.F. robbed the hospital two years earlier. In some respects the robbery was like paying ransom to prevent a kidnapping.

I thought of that fact as I prepared to reply to their letter. It was sixteen days since Debbie had been kidnapped. When I had answered the first letter, I thought God would deliver Debbie immediately if I but trusted Him and demonstrated that trust by not giving in to the demands. Twelve days had passed since then. Could I justify risking her life any longer?

The reasoning behind our earlier decision was pretty sound after all, I concluded. I weighed the ransom demands of the E.L.F. against those of the Bible: Jesus came "not to be served but to serve, and to give His life a ransom for many." Disobedience and pride separated man from God's love. Acting as a mediator, Jesus had paid the full penalty of sin and His ransom reunited men to God. How ironical, I thought, that I should be asked to pay ransom for Debbie when in Christ she already had life and freedom. The ransom that the E.L.F. demanded—what could it do? It could not give life, it would not insure E.L.F. faithfulness. It would bring future difficulty rather than secure peace.

As mediator of the ransom, I was bankrupt with nothing to offer. But Christ had mediated the full payment of ransom to God. In Him were hope and peace, authority and power—power to bring Debbie out of her captors' hands, power to overrule the fear of the E.L.F. that lurked within me, and power to write them a bold reply. I lifted my pen and without any hesitation wrote:

We have received your letter dated 6. 10. 74. By what you say, you must not have received any of our letters. We send to you, with this letter, our letter from all missions in Eritrea. We repeat now what we said in our first letter to you.

1) We will not consider any demands until Mrs. Debbie is safely returned to us.

2) No money will ever be paid for any missionaries who have come to Eritrea to help the people.

Now concerning your letter to us, we have several things we should have to say to you.

1) You say that the case of Mrs. Debbie is different than that of the Tenneco men. But when you demand so many things you show to us that you think we are like the Tenneco Oil Company. Even if we wanted to send so much money, it is more than we could send even by selling all of the hospital.

2) You say that you are concerned because 352 Eritrean people have died of cholera. But if you were concerned, you would not kill Miss Anna and kidnap Mrs. Debbie. Because of these actions, all mission clinics and hospitals in Eritrea are closed. Now the people cannot have any help for their diseases.

3) We are very concerned about the many deaths because of cholera. God has sent us to Eritrea to help the people, and we want to help them but your actions so far mean that we cannot help them.

These are the ways that many missions are helping the people of Eritrea:

1) Clinics, hospitals and schools in many places: Aicota, Afabet, Massawa, Tessenei, Ghinda. All of these places can help the people especially when cholera is breaking out.

2) In Afabet the people now have enough sweet water. There is a large windmill that is ready to be set up on a sweet well, but this cannot be until Mrs. Debbie is released and the safety of all missions is insured. The large dam cannot be finished before rainy season unless next week the work can be started again. The work cannot start until Mrs. Debbie is released and all missions will be safe.

3) In Ghinda we had medicine to control cholera for 20,000 people. The week that Miss Anna was killed and Mrs. Debbie was kidnapped, we had planned to go out into the country to

give medicine and injections. Now because of your actions, many people have died that did not need to die.

4) All missions would gladly send medical people into the country to help the people. But medical people will not be sent out as hostages, and they will not go unless they may go freely into the country without harm.

We are now asking you to release Mrs. Debbie immediately and give us a written letter assuring our safety so that we may go to give medical care to the Eritrean people. We want very much to help the people of Eritrea. Now we ask you a question. Are you wanting to help the people of Eritrea by allowing us to give them medical care?

We hope to have as your quick reply: 1) the release of Mrs. Debbie, and 2) a letter stating that no mission will ever be attacked again.

> Thank you,
> (Signed) Karl Dortzbach

Ben Motis had suggested that we carefully list all the benefits missions had afforded the people. Thus we made a contrast to what the E.L.F. letter said; they talked about concern—we showed our solutions to the problems.

After I had finished writing I gave the letter to Jim to read. Our procedure was a regular one. With the exception of the first letter, only two or three of us would actually do the writing and approving, and then the others would just read what was done. Having more than three of us seemed unnecessary. Art was busy learning to do the mission and hospital books; Gil, Sandra, and Greet worked nearly every day at a rehabilitation clinic in Asmara.

When I took my letter to the others to read, the reaction was rather mixed. They were thankful that the Lord had given me strength to be bold—in fact, they wondered if the letter might not be too bold—but why had we asked for a letter insuring the missions' safety? Did we trust the E.L.F. more than God for safety? After all, had they not promised after the previous hospital raid never to disturb the mission again?

"From their past record," I explained, "such an assurance is only as good as they want it to be. The real reason for our request is to make our bargaining position as strong as possible." We would not pay ransom, but more than that, we would not even make a promise to return to Ghinda unless the E.L.F. themselves were willing to concede.

The E.L.F. rendezvous would be Friday, June 14. Saleh left again with the letter. "This time," he told us, "it is not so far from Ghinda. I will go and return in a day."

Waiting always made me nervous. I began to worry about the strong tone of our letter. After all I really had blamed the E.L.F. for the death of many people; in essence I had told them that their kind of "concern" was more harmful than helpful. I wanted to take the letter back and soften it; but the time for that was passed. Later in the afternoon I wrote letters home to help shed the heaviness that seized me. Father's Day would be the following Sunday, and I wanted to tell my father that at least I was thinking of him. I could not hide my discouragement:

> . . . such days as these deepen discouragement, and it becomes more than a little difficult to have genuine love in my heart for those who have done such things. Yet Christ loved us while we were yet sinful. It makes the depth of His love even more unfathomable.
>
> Before I forget it—Happy Father's Day! Sorry I can't send you a card, or even a little gift. You are much too far away for that, but still I hear your words of comfort, and know the Scripture that soothes the most festered wound. I feel your hand on my shoulder and know your voice in prayer. Many years have taught me those things, and now I can but give God the praise. It's still true, you know, and times like these will only prove it more so—"Seek first His Kingdom and His righteousness and all these things [all life's needs] shall be added to you."
>
> Seeking and finding His all
in all,
>
> Your Son

135

The rendezvous several miles outside of Ghinda was kept by Saleh, who carried not only our letter but also a copy of the general mission letter to the village shumes. We had included it not because it was to the E.L.F., but because it would convey the pressure on the shumes. We hoped the double-punch of two letters would jar the E.L.F. into a favorable response.

We expected Saleh to return sometime Friday afternoon or evening, and he did. By the time he reached Ghinda, however, the Asmara road had long been closed for the night, and he could only telephone us to say he was back. "I don't know anything," he told us, "but I have something for you." We assumed he meant another letter, which he would bring to us the next morning.

Starting with the ring of my alarm clock at seven that Saturday, I was drawn into a conflict. Did I dare believe that God not only could but would bring back a positive letter? Could I force God to do something just because I "believed" it? Surely not, but nonetheless I was confident that the coming letter bore good news. The captors could have killed Debbie long before, but they did not. Instead they looked after her needs. I felt also that many people who were concerned about the kidnapping were wondering if God was as able as we claimed—certainly God would vindicate His own name!

Not long after breakfast Saleh came with the letter crumpled up in his shoe. I opened it quickly . . . it had five full pages. Letting out a soft whistle, I then called my "advisers" around me. The letter got down to business immediately:

The E.L.F. executive committee wants to give the following points in reply to the six points of the mission. 1) You say no money will ever be paid for any missionaries, but it has no relation with our requests. 2) You say the Eritrean Liberation Front asks so much that Mrs. Debbie's case is like Tenneco, but it is a different case and for this we want to clarify that Tenneco personnels release is depending upon millions of dollars ransom and by that the following requests for Mrs. Debbie are very low. 3) The week Mrs. Anna was killed you say that you had planned to give anti-cholera medicines. We do not believe that you had the plan of going into the country to defend cholera. 4) You say many people have died because of our actions. Whose fault was it that they died before the Ghinda operation? We say that it is not by our reason that the people died. We always calculate and work for the safety of our Eritrean people. 5) You ask if we are willing to help cure the people. O.K. We are going to give you allowance to cure the people and from this you may see that something happens after the Ghinda operation for the safety of our people. 6) You request: a. the release of Mrs. Debbie and, b. a letter saying the mission will never be attacked again. a. Release of Mrs. Debbie is very easy. b. O.K. We are going to give you insurance according to our law.

"Notice" for the above sixth reply.

We are going to fulfill all the above points if the mission agrees with the following Eritrean Liberation Front points: Our last demand is the following

1) We decrease $62,500 dollars. Then you are going to pay $12,500 dollars.
2) Cholera medicines as it was told in our letter.
3) You must have to say the following in the Radio B.B.C. and Voice of America.
   (a). Mrs. Debbie is going to be released.
   (b). Eritrean Liberation Front asks excuse in the death of the late Mrs. Anna.
   (c). Eritrean Liberation Front requests cholera medicine as ransom of release Mrs. Debbie.

By only the above mentioned requests we are going to release Mrs. Debbie automatically. And after her release, you should have to bring the following things:
   (a). Five microphones.
   (b). Five typewriters.
   (c). Two duplicators.
   (d). Malaria medicines $5,000 dollars.

All of the above requests is going to be paid after Mrs. Debbie's release and for this you should have to bring guarantee. And it is after you finish the four last requests that Eritrean Liberation Front gives allowance and makes full insurance for all missionaries.

1. Letter dated 1 June 1974 signed by four missions came to us attached with your letter. And we are not going to reply for it, because it is non-political letter. Therefore, such things we are not going to accept a second time by the American Evangelical Mission.
2. And it is very risky if you spent more time in Mrs. Debbie's case.
3. And all things written in our letter must be finished within a week. If you add more time and spend it unreasonably, it is very risky on her life and another punishment will follow.

Executive Committee

I reread the last sentences. Twice the E.L.F. had warned me that any deviation would be risky for Debbie. They had lowered the demands by $62,500, but what remained was still far more than I could ever pay. I knew, of course, that the E.L.F. were simply keeping pressure on us to meet the demands. But I knew too that they could well commit one more horrid, heartless murder. "If you add more time," they had threatened, ". . . another punishment will follow."

After we had all read the letter, it was important to question Saleh about the men's reaction to our letter, their manner, and their spirit.

"Adam is a hard man," Saleh emphasized. "When he read the letter from the missions, his eyes got small like this"—he narrowed his eyes to slits—"and he was angry. Oooh, Mr. Karl, they were very angry, I tell you I was afraid." He went on to describe their reaction more fully. Apparently, the mission letter had hit them squarely and hurt their pride, but still they became quite angry. Happily, however, Saleh said they had simply refused to discuss the letter with him.

Saleh knew nothing about the contents of the letter that he had carried to us. Adam and Yakob had encouraged him only by saying that Mrs. Debbie would be released soon. Such encouragement did not seem to correlate with the letter.

Suddenly, I remembered my thoughts earlier that week after we had received the first demand letter. The Executive Committee were "bargaining"! Indeed, they were playing their part well. They had lowered the demands considerably, yet tried to bluff us into thinking that we must act quickly in complying with their revised demands. I could not know just how far we could push them, nor at what point they would stand firm on their demands. Nor could I, of course, be sure that they really would not carry out their threat, except that Saleh had been encouraged about a release.

Saleh would have to return to Ghinda that afternoon. Since he had scheduled another E.L.F. rendezvous for Sunday morning, the next day, I had no time to waste in making a reply. But what would I reply? How could I say the same thing over again?

"Any suggestions?" I asked Jim and Ben.

"You'll just have to say it again," Jim said with a kind of frustrated grin. "Answer each point of their letter as they did with yours."

"I think you ought to say what Jesus said to the Pharisees and crowd that wanted to kill him," suggested Ben. " 'For which of my good works do you seek to kill me?' Repeat some of the things that missions have done and then put the question to them."

There was wisdom in their suggestions. The thought of using Jesus' own irrefutable words to confront the E.L.F. leaders excited me. I picked up my pen and began the letter. Following the E.L.F. pattern, I listed the four main points of their letter consecutively and added our response to each:

. . . 1) When you demand $12,500 and many other things that cost money, you show that you do not understand the policy of the American Evangelical Mission and all other missions. We say again, no money or anything that costs money will ever be paid to ransom or blackmail any missionary or missionary organization. Paying ransom and blackmail is against our moral and religious teaching. The only money we will give you is to pay for food that Mrs. Debbie has eaten while you hold her hostage.

2) You do not believe that our hospital had planned to go out

into the country to defend cholera. In that, you say that we lie. If you insist on such a thing, then you would not believe us even when you would see the boxes of vaccination that are still in Ghinda. If you do not believe us, it is because you do not want to believe us. But if you say such a thing, you show that you do not want the people of Eritrea to be helped from cholera.

I was being bold, but there was no time to play games. I had to strike at the center of their thinking. In essence their letter said we were lying. Such an accusation was a serious offense in Eritrean minds. Their accusation had to be exposed as an attempt to hide the truth. I continued:

3) You make three things that we should have to say on the radio. But we will not lie in anything we say. We cannot say that you are releasing Mrs. Debbie for *only* cholera medicine when you also demand many other things from us.

If you release Mrs. Debbie immediately without harm, we will say to the radio and press all true things that happen. We only refer to you as the Eritrean Liberation Front because that is your name.

4) If we do not obey your demands, you threaten to harm Mrs. Debbie and make other punishments. Then we must ask you a question. Do you want all of the world to know that you harmed or killed a nurse who was pregnant with her first son? Do you want the world to know that you harm and punish people who come to help the Eritrean people? We do not think that you want the world to know this. You have been known as an organization that wants to help the people and as an organization that is kind, even to those whom it captures.

Now, if you harm Mrs. Debbie or make other punishments, then all of the world will know your organization as one that has no concern for the people who come with peace in their hearts.

We think that you have concern for the people but if you truly have concern for the people, you should immediately release Mrs. Debbie and give safety to all missions to continue helping the people.

5) Now we must ask you a question. The missions have done many good deeds for the people of Eritrea. For which one of these

good deeds do you now harm us? For which of these good deeds do you demand money and equipment?

The missions have helped the people of Eritrea by giving schools, clinics, hospitals, water and community development.

And now you say that you always calculate and work for the safety of the people. But now people have died from cholera because the hospitals and clinics are not open. Many more people will die if these do not open again. People will be without water, education, medicines. If you want the safety and good for the people, you should have to release Mrs. Debbie and give us a letter signed by the Executive Committee that these things will never happen again. Then we will be able to help your people again.

Now we should review our important things.

1) We ask you to release Mrs. Debbie immediately and give us a letter to never harm missions again.
2) We will not pay any money or goods for any missionary.
3) We will say in the press and radio everything true about the case.
4) We want to help the Eritrean people in fighting against diseases, but we cannot do it while you hold Mrs. Debbie hostage and give threats to us.

We hope for your quick reply.

Laying down my pen, I passed the letter around as usual. Jim agreed with it. It tossed the matter back to the E.L.F. where it belonged. Ben read it next; he too felt it expressed what we wanted to say. Our hope and confidence were in God, and our letter made it clear that paying ransom was something we would not do.

After I had rewritten the letter on official mission stationery and carefully placed the mission stamp after my signature, I gave it to Saleh. He did not think he would be able to make the Sunday morning rendezvous personally because the days of walking had left his muscles too sore to stand or sit, much less walk. Even though the E.L.F. leaders were to be only a short distance away, he felt that another messenger could carry the letter just as well. He would find someone else.

As soon as Saleh drove off with the letter, I began to have second thoughts about that one too. Such a bold letter could induce negative reactions. We had not budged even the slightest in our position and were requiring the E.L.F. to do all the bending and changing. I wondered if that were such a smart move. The leaders' response to the general mission letter had been one of great anger; my current letter characterized their threat as unmanly—how would they react to that? We had ignored their threat, yet suddenly it hovered like a guillotine triggered into action.

Sunday, June 16, should have been a day of rest—rest not just from normal physical labors but also from mental stress. My rest, however, was fitful. At times I would wonder if Debbie's life would yet be lost. At other times I would concentrate upon God's promises, recognizing that for three weeks He had led me, given us wisdom, protected Debbie, and answered a thousand prayers for different things. Most of Sunday, however, was just waiting.

Monday morning I tried to keep busy, but in the afternoon I felt the need to spend some time alone. I reflected upon the many things I had learned again and again during the last twenty days, and prayed. I then read through some of the letters that had started to trickle in after the paralyzing postal strike. They were letters of encouragement from many who had been so close to us at home. Thousands were praying. Prayer chains had been formed in many churches, information was sent out to alumni of Wheaton College and friends of Westminster Seminary. I even had cards and letters from people in other parts of the world who never knew of us before. Typically, they would begin by saying, "I hope by the time you get this Debbie is with you. . . ." She was not, but I began to understand the tremendous source of power that had been gathered. Prayer was the language of God's Kingdom. Through prayer all of God's powerful promises were unleashed, for He listened and was faithful to His children.

I reread a letter from my father. It was dated May 31, the Friday after the hospital raid. He too reflected upon the several passages of Scripture that had brought comfort and peace to my heart. His closing words reminded me of God's power:

May you know the bright shining stars of sufficient grace in the night of your soul's experience as you re-commit the dearest in life to your Lord. And as this story unfolds, however long it takes and through whatever path you must follow, how good to know our Good Shepherd goes before us in all our ways. How real is our Lord in such an hour, how sufficient is His gracious help!

The sufficiency of God's help was to be challenged that very night. After an evening at the mission apartment, I returned to my room at the S.I.M. Ben Motis came to give me a letter that Saleh had brought while I was out. It was an unexpected reply. As he handed me the folded letter without an envelope, Ben had not looked anxious, just defeated and quiet.

Late Friday afternoon, June 14, Bekeet came from his village, escorting a visitor.

The visitor was ushered into the hut and greeted warmly by my guards; I eyed him carefully. He wore a green cap, and his work-shirt-green uniform seemed relatively new with not even a single patch on it. He lifted a box off his back, plunked it into a corner, and breathing an exhausted sigh, stretched out to rest. Dark skin did not mask his flushed face, and perspiration poured profusely down his neck.

"*Shahee?*" I asked, remembering my pledge to make tea for all visitors.

"Yes," he answered in English, and I went outside to gather sticks.

While fanning the fire, I listened intently to the conversation inside the hut. When I heard Adam's name mentioned, I fanned more vigorously with excitement. The tea bubbled over, and I poured it into my glass and took it into the visitor. As I sat down on my cot, I could suppress my questions no longer.

"Have you come from Adam?" I asked.

A young "shepherd" boy, holding a "walking stick" like his father's, sits forlornly on the hospital steps.

"Yes," he answered.

My whole body throbbed in anticipation as I stumbled over the next question:

"Wh—what does he say?"

"Wait till after tea, then we will tell you everything," Sayeed said. He paused briefly, then resumed his reading of letters carried to him by the visitor.

Shaken, I took out my embroidery and tried to force myself to sew, but I gave up when my eyes failed to focus on the stitches. Would I see Karl soon?

The visitor, whose name I learned was Dawit, slurped down his tea, and then, pointing to the box he had plunked into the corner, announced that it was for me.

"For me?" I echoed in disbelief. Not waiting for his answer, I knelt beside it and began to untie the ropes. I was not prepared for what lay inside.

On top were three dresses. Clean dresses! Colorful dresses! One was dark blue and white checkered with big pockets, one was yellow with big tulips decorating the front, and one was light blue, flowered, and with a full skirt. I lifted them to my face and enjoyed their fresh laundered feeling. The dresses were not my own. A familiar scent of perfume lingered on them—Beverly Miner's, Jim's wife. I went through the box and pulled out a clean pair of underwear (what a luxury to have two pairs!), a bar of hexachlorophene soap that I recognized was from the hospital, two toothbrushes (someone must have thought I really needed them!), two tubes of toothpaste, one of which was three-fourths used, bottles of vitamins and calcium tablets and water purification tablets, a large white towel, a washcloth with a capital K embroidered on the front which was unmistakably Karl's. The bottom of the box contained food items: more canned meat(!), canned tomato paste, spaghetti, a can of powdered milk, and a horn of cheese; a bowl, knife, fork, and spoon were also included. I gasped at the last items in the treasure box: two Cadbury chocolate bars.

My eyes brimmed with tears. I returned to sit on the cot, the

145

contents of the box spread out before me. I browsed through the items again, and then searched them more carefully. One thing was missing . . . one thing I was sure Karl would have put in. I turned over every item, examined the dress pockets, and searched the empty box. There was no Bible. I knew Karl would have put the Bible in *first.* And the dresses! They were not mine. Not even the toothbrush I left hanging in our bathroom had been sent. Karl could not have packed the box. He would have been more careful. Where was Karl? No letter from him had been included. Was he even alive? Had he left the country? Or had the E.L.F. shot him?

"Does anybody know *anything* about my husband?" I lashed out at the men.

"He is fine," Dawit answered. "You know Saleh? He gave me the box. He said your husband is fine."

Could I believe him? Why had the box not contained anything from Karl? I looked through the items again as I returned them to the box. On the back of one of the chocolate bars the following words were penciled in large sprawling letters: "To dear Aunt Debbie, Love Ruthie."

They were the first words of affection I had had in weeks. The men in the hut looked on as I buried my wet cheeks in my hands. I thought of Ruthie, the Miners' seven-year-old daughter. She had often felt rejected in Ghinda, since the only available playmates were boys. Her only school classmate was her brother, and she sorely lacked fun times with girls her age. To ease her loneliness, the two of us would meet together weekly on Monday evenings for Ruthie's "Special Time." It was an evening all her own to learn embroidery, to make Christmas gifts, or to bake. Only several weeks earlier she had planned a surprise supper for her family. Together we had spent the entire afternoon in preparation: making pizza, cutting up carrot sticks, and beating homemade chocolate ice cream. I reread her message. If she could only know the "Special Time" she was giving me right then. Chocolate bars were one of my "pregnancy passions," as Karl had dubbed them. After weeks of canned meat and rice I had forgotten how chocolate tasted.

I looked closer at the can of powdered milk as I went over every item in the box for the fourth or fifth time. It was powdered infant formula! I giggled. It was hardly the way I had expected the Lord to answer my prayer of the last three days. The goat herders no longer brought milk. When I had asked the E.L.F. if they could obtain some, they merely shook their heads. If none were brought, there was nothing they could do. I had been praying specifically for more goat's milk, since it was my best source of protein and necessary for the development of the baby.

I could not believe everything in the box was mine. The chocolate bars were rather misshapen, evidence of melting and rehardening many times during the overland trip. Unable to wait longer, I tore open the outer wrapping and tinfoil inside and indulged in the ecstasy of satisfying my "pregnancy passion." I cherished each bite. Wishing to draw out such pleasure, I bit off only a small amount and securely wrapped up the rest. To protect the chocolate from melting or from being devoured by ants or the friendly, bold mouse that visited the hut frequently, I emptied the first-aid kit and placed the bars as well as the vitamins inside for safekeeping.

Sayeed still held the letters sent to him through Dawit. I examined his face for a clue as to their contents.

He did the unexpected: He handed me one of the letters.

Eritrean Liberation Front   6–12–74
Executive Committee

To Mrs. Debbie

Hereby we want to acknowledge you about what is going on about your case for release.

1.) At first when we were planning the operation of kidnapping in Ghinda, it was not our plan to kidnap you and Mrs. Anna. Our plan was to take out the doctor in order to examine about the distributed disease cholera and if it was possible to give us as an aid medicines anti the disease. But through some tactical mistakes our guerrela unit brought as kidnapped you and late Mrs. Anna.

2.) Now we know that you are not in a good condition and we could also imagine that you suffers alot about the condition you were found in it. But you must to help us in economize the foods which is found with you and secondly by tolerate all things which is facing to you.

3.) At last we like to inform you that recently we start relation with the mission and we requests from them anti cholera and malaria medicines. We asked them such ransoms because cholera and malaria disease is terribly distributed in this district and we hope the mission would give us reply soonly. And after they brought these requests we are going to release you automatically.

May the Almighty God fulfill all our wishes for all those who believes Him.

Thank you
Yours faithfully
The Executive Committee
Eritrean Liberation Front

The letter left me puzzled, ambivilant. I reread it many more times, pausing at each point. I did not find it comforting that Anna's death was called a "tactical mistake." I found it only revolting. I was thankful Gil was not in my place, that that part of their operation had been bungled. But what did they really want from us anyway? I remembered Berhane's words of the week before: "We want the whole world to know about the E.L.F. You see, this way, because of your case, they will know we are trying to help our people."

The second point in the letter left me feeling utterly helpless. "Economize" and "tolerate" conjured up pictures of long months ahead filled with uncertainty, boredom, depression, and disease. The foodstuffs would perhaps last a week. How long would it be before another box came?

Point three made me wonder if I could believe anything I was told. The hospital raid and Anna's murder must have been done for some other reason than simply medicines.

I pondered for a long time on the last statement: "May the Almighty God fulfill all our wishes for all those who believes Him." The men unquestionably respected God, but what did they know of His love? I marveled at the fulfillment of that love shown to me: a new box of supplies, a chocolate bar, a new dress. Later that night His love was demonstrated in another way: Dawit slept in the hut between Sayeed and myself.

Saturday morning a donkey deposited its burden of waterskins early. A few days before Sayeed had given me a small aluminum pan to use "just for your cooking." It would also serve as a water container. I was eager to have enough water to brush my teeth and to wash myself, but even though I had toothpaste and a toothbrush, it would not be simple to clean my teeth. The impure water would have turned healthful toothbrushing into a hazard for parasitic infection.

As usual the water was murky and thick with unwanted particles. Using a piece of gauze from the first-aid kit, I attempted to filter the debris as I poured an estimated quart of water into my pan. Then I dropped one of the water purification tablets into it and sat down to wait the twenty minutes for the tablet to take effect. I was so anxious to have my first drink that I ticked off each minute. Finally, filling my glass to the top, I gulped down the water. The goatskins had kept the water relatively cool, and while it had a mineral, dusty taste, it was refreshing. Partially filling my glass again, I left the hut with toothbrush and paste in hand. After three weeks I could feel civilized again.

But I soon had a practical problem. Having once purified the water, how could I keep it clean? The pan had no lid or covering to keep out the dust from the floor and also the healthy ant population. So, scrounging through my food box, I discovered a piece of plastic suitable as a cover.

Having solved my water problem, I planned my day: first task was to tidy my corner of the hut. As I swept the dirt floor, aired my sleeping bag, and rearranged my food supply, my mind flitted back to the time eight months earlier when Karl and I had worked in the famine area of Ethiopia. We had traveled to the provinces south of Eritrea to relieve personnel of other missions. Hundreds of famine victims had migrated out of distant isolated villages to the main road in search of grain and help. Masses of rag-swathed, fly-swarmed bodies had stretched out before us. It was a sea of haggard, gaunt faces attached to remnants of human flesh. Each one had clung to their only possessions: a rusty tin can, a walking stick, a tattered garment. They had clung as if those belongings were their last touch with reality as they slowly slipped out of life. They had huddled in the corner of an open feeding compound, calling that corner theirs. I too had my corner of the hut. It was mine. The box was mine. That was all I had, and I protected it.

Going to my cot, I picked up the embroidery again and sat down in my corner to begin a new verse. It was to be an anniversary gift for my parents who had celebrated their twenty-sixth wedding anniversary that week. I could clearly picture their twenty-fifth anniversary the year before. Into the room had crowded numerous friends, church members, and not least of all, the nine of us children. We could not afford to give our parents an expensive celebration, a trip to Europe, or a silver tea service, but we wanted to return the gift they had given to us—love.

With faltering voices each family member had shared what our mom and dad meant to us. I recalled my twin brother, Tim. Crippled with cerebral palsy, he had stood a bit wobbly, and then with slow, deliberate speech he told of the years he remembered, with mom and dad faithfully prodding and encouraging him as he learned to walk without assistance. His persistence in learning to walk had enabled him to be self-supporting with a full-time job. The rest of us had taken our turns to speak, down to my youngest ten-year-old brother.

I wondered how my parents had spent their twenty-sixth anniversary? With a prayer of thanksgiving, I knew that they had rested in God's peace. They had lived and taught me that peace. In and out, back and forth, I stitched the verse:

When I prepared for bed that night, I decided to set aside one of my new dresses as a nightgown. It was the most comfortable and loose-fitting. My uniform was too tight to wear. Even the guards had commented earlier, "Mrs. Debbie, before we did not believe you were pregnant, but now we are sure you are." I slipped into the dress and then into my sleeping bag.

I was jolted out of my sleep in the middle of the night by steps inside the hut. The shuffling feet were Sayeed's. I peered at him through the darkness, my body frozen with fear. No one else was sleeping in the hut, since Dawit had left that day.

My eyes were glued to Sayeed's every movement. He stood on his mat an endless length of time and then sauntered outside, unaware that I was awake. Returning to the hut, he reached for the strap dangling from an overhead log. His gun!

"Sayeed! What do you want?" My trembling voice penetrated the silence.

Surprised, he looked at me, his gun clutched in his fingers. "Never mind," came his rough retort. "Never mind."

I cried frantically to God with my eyes squeezed shut and my body plastered to the bed. Was I again in the midst of "the valley of the shadow of death"? I wrestled for control of my fear but gave up, admitting all my fears to that great Shepherd who promised to be with me. Sayeed stood there for a long time as the night passed slowly. Finally I heard him shuffle back to his mat.

Sunday morning . . . My whole body ached in despair as I stepped out of the sleeping bag. Would I yet die in that place of rest? I went outside and headed for the rock, which had become more of a resting place than my cot.

I was lost in bitterness, frantic with fear. Picking up a stick, I drew circles aimlessly in the dusty ground. Then looking up, I was surprised to see a visitor. Beady black eyes, only inches away, sparkled in the sunlight. While basking in the sun, he worked at

151

his morning exercises, doing pushups. At once he stopped, cocked his head sharply to the side, and glared at me. It was a lizard! Without really wanting to, I laughed out loud. As the lizard continued its antics, I laughed the louder, forgetting my fears. God knew I needed to laugh right then. How long it had been since I actually laughed out loud! The lizard, frightened by my reaction, slid into the crack of a rock. As it reappeared and sprinted from rock to rock, I was prompted to write in my notebook:

Am I like that lizard
That just scurried in front of me?
He looked so curious, cautious—
Perhaps even worried as he jerked
His head from side to side
Before he buried himself into
The crack of a rock.

Or am I like those goats
On that hillside there?
They easily glide across rugged rock
Up on cliffs—seemingly so
Monumentous.

Lord, make my feet like hind's feet,
As Your Word says—
Sure-footed, steady, secure
Ever in Your path, rough though it be.
Take away the scrutinizing, worried look
Of the lizard—
Do not allow me to hide
From lessons You want to teach me
In these mountains.
Help me to know Your freedom.

Returning to camp, I found the men diving into their noon rationing of porridge. Bekeet had just arrived with water and food. Since I did not feel hungry, I laid down on my cot. Acting on a wild thought, I asked Sayeed if I might listen to his radio. Surprisingly, he shoved it toward me. Turning the dial from one strange flutter of words to another, I thought back to the previous Sunday and to the message I had heard. I had asked for the radio since then, but learned with great disappointment that the time of that program conflicted with the Arabic news. Not expecting to locate anything worth listening, I continued to turn the dial haphazardly.

My ears picked up a strand of music. It was not the high-pitched wail of an Arabic song, or the repetitious drone of a Tigrinya melody, but the smooth resonance of violins, cellos, and woodwinds. As I listened, I identified the composition as Debussy's *Rêverie*. I feasted on every note as the music swelled to climactic crescendos and subsided to restful lulls. The last note sounded and the announcer chimed in. It had been the Philadelphia Orchestra, with Eugene Ormandy! Only the year before Karl and I had sat high in the balcony of the Academy of Music in Philadelphia, watching the artful hands of that great master conduct the orchestra.

The music brought vivid memories of another historic evening: my first date with Karl seven years earlier in the colonial-style chapel of Wheaton College. The Vienna Philharmonic had performed. And so had Karl—at his very best in trying to impress the girl he had met only several days before. It was a date I had accepted somewhat reluctantly. From then on, every casual meeting with Karl had brought a barrage of unwanted and unaccepted invitations to social functions.

I had thought of him blindly as a scrawny mountain lover from Colorado. Meanwhile, upperclassmen kept me busy. One day I began to see that my romanticized ideal, a superficial man with glamorous accomplishments and glorified dates, was not the man I should be seeking. Rather, the true ideal was someone who would show concern for others, someone who on Sunday mornings would take effort to help a mentally retarded child draw pictures of the Sunday school lesson, someone who would listen sympathetically to the problems of an ailing nursing home patient, someone who would spend a lifetime not only preaching, but demonstrating the love of Christ.

We were to become friends, sharing in like interests and extracurricular activities; then lovers, left lonely with eight hundred miles between us while we completed our last two years of college; then three years of marriage—and left lonely again with foreign mountain wilderness and a militant band of men forcing us apart. It was inconceivably real.

The afternoon advanced more quickly than I realized. Soon the fire was prepared for supper's tea. Digging down into my box, I pulled out the same can of luncheon meat I had opened the previous day. Experience had taught me that an opened can would last only two days before spoiling. I could never work up a ferocious appetite and consequently had to make smaller more frequent meals out of it. That night's specialty would be luncheon meat entree with sliced cheese on cookie, baby formula mixed with fizzled mountain stream water, topped with a square of chocolate for dessert. Such a menu deserved a more genteel dining atmosphere. Thinking back to a book I had read several years before, *Hidden Art* by Edith Schaeffer, I explored my "hidden creativity" and came up with a wooden crate spread with a colorful striped tablecloth from my yard of material, set with knife, fork, spoon, bowl, napkin (also from the material). Seating myself by the soft glowing light of the fading campfire, I dined in thanksgiving on the third Sunday of my captivity.

Two nights passed without any interruptions in my sleep, but on Tuesday night, June 18, I was again startled awake.

It was after the camp had settled that the sound of clicking hoofs split the night. Sayeed was the first to leap to his feet. Clutching and cocking his pistol, he went outside.

Who would visit at that hour? There was not even a moon to illuminate the rugged path.

Left: Debbie holds a famine victim in Wollo Province, south of Eritrea.

Below: Karl speaks to waiting famine victims about Jesus, the Bread of Life.

As I opened the letter that Ben Motis had handed me, my father's words were still in my mind: "How real is our Lord in such an hour, how sufficient is His gracious help!" I wondered if the letter without an envelope had already been read. The single sheet of paper had some peculiar letters and number at the top. What they meant was unclear, but the date was clearly June 16. It had been written the previous day, undoubtedly during the rendezvous with the E.L.F. I devoured the contents of the short note:

Eritrean Liberation Front
Executive Committee
   To American Evangelical Mission, Ghinda
   The Eritrean Liberation Front received your letter dated 15 June 1974.
   We understand from your letter that you did not believe or apply our instructions from our letter 6/14/74 which the main point or idea was our "last demand." Therefore, for the reason you refuse to give your real or wanted reply, the mission is going to be asked [to assume] responsibility for this new error.

Eritrean Liberation Front
Executive Committee

I sat down and stared at the last line. The meaning was unmistakable.

As I folded the letter, a sudden chill struck me: Perhaps I had misunderstood the letter! It must be simply a note to tell me that I should think twice about the previous letter because it contained the final demands. Or was the letter a prank? The peculiar letters and number at the top did not appear "official."

The truth was too brutal to take. I simply *had* to find another meaning. Try as I might, however, I had to face it. Our letter had been rejected. The E.L.F. were not just bargaining; they did mean to carry out their threats, and they were telling us we were responsible for the new error. Again I tried to avoid the obvious. They must have used the wrong word, I reasoned. They meant only that negotiations would be broken off. After all, that was what happened to Tenneco when their replies had been rejected.

But I knew that the very brevity of the E.L.F. letter meant much more than just the severance of our correspondence. It was not just the end of that phase of our dealing. It was the end of life . . . Debbie's life. My bargaining made me responsible for the death of my own wife.

The days and weeks of loneliness, of waiting, of praying, of encouragement, of hope . . . suddenly despair. It would have been better, I thought, if Debbie had been killed with Anna, then it would have been over. I would have expected it at that time and understood. Had it happened three weeks earlier, God would have given much strength and power to help me in my distress. But God had encouraged me with word that she was alive. Scripture had filled me with hope and promise. Through the prayers of perhaps thousands I had been raised above despair to an eager anticipation of her return. The fall was bitter and hard. What was God trying to teach me?

"The darkest part of the night," Ben's voice spoke softly, "is just before dawn."

Tears filled the corners of my eyes. He *had* read the letter before me; he knew. I bit the sides of my tongue to keep my tears back.

After all that the Lord had helped me through, I wanted to be strong. I wanted more than anything for Ben to see me taking patiently and thankfully what the Lord had given. I did not want to be filled with bitterness, for I knew God never promised that Debbie would be given to me again. Rather, He promised to be near me.

My father had reminded me of the sufficiency of God's help to keep me from falling into despair; yet grief flooded me. What was left? What could I do? I had been facing the possibility of permanent separation from Debbie since that fateful Monday. Loneliness was no longer a possibility; it seemed an indisputable fact. I would return to the States without a wife. In our marriage she had completed me; without Debbie I would not have that second voice with which to be objective. Her spontaneity would be gone, her radiance, her loving care—I would be without any of it.

I needed strength, something to grab ahold of that was sure and changeless. I turned again to God, who alone had been my strength and hope during the ordeal. I could hope in none other because there was no hope in any other. Ben walked with me to the deserted living room that adjoined a common kitchen and dining room. Together we sat and poured out our hearts to our Lord and King.

"Father God, even now I know that You are able to bring Debbie back," I prayed, "but if she does not return, then give me the strength to bear it . . . and please give me the faith to walk confidently in Your promises and power."

When we finished, we walked back to our rooms; everyone else had long since gone to bed. As I returned to my room, I worried about many things. I knew nothing of the circumstances surrounding the writing of the letter. That would have to wait until the next morning when Saleh would fill me in. Meanwhile, there was the question of whether or not another rendezvous had been scheduled. Also, what had Yakob and Adam said after they wrote the letter? Had they intended it to be a scare tactic? If they had, it was working fine.

As I swung my feet into the stony bed, I anticipated years yet to come. I would always be sleeping alone. No longer would I be having the warmth and expressed love so often enjoyed with Debbie. I lay shivering nervously, wondering about the next step. I would have to wait for a while before I went back to the States. Perhaps Debbie's body would be found soon, or some word would come from a shepherd, confirming the letter's dire prediction. But while I lay there worrying, I became aware of my unbelief. I showed no confidence that God really could bring Debbie back even then, no confidence that I would be able to bear the pain of loneliness and separation.

I reminisced. Three years really were not that long a time. Three years ago I had been anticipating marriage with all its joys and struggles. Nearly three years of learning, loving, enjoying, and developing had passed. I could not very well count those years for nothing! They had been intense growing times. Growing in my love for God as I grew to love Debbie more . . . growing to take responsibilities . . . growing in an awareness of God's great power. The years of marriage had been wonderful—exciting and beautiful, not dull and difficult.

The contents of the letter were uppermost in my mind when I awoke. It was Tuesday morning, June 18. As I went to breakfast, everyone wanted to know about the letter. They expected a positive answer: to tell them otherwise was not going to be easy.

"It is all over," I said. "The last letter had their final demands and now they are making us responsible for their next mistake." The hurricanelike blast traveled quickly. Soon everyone began to look at me sorrowfully, wondering what they could say.

Instead of everyone's condolences, what I really wanted was to hear the details from Saleh. When finally he came to the compound, he was disappointing. He had nothing to add, since he had not delivered our last reply letter. The messenger had told him only that the E.L.F. leaders took the letter without comment. The reply was their only response.

As though that were not bad enough, Saleh's words, "He forgot to make another appointment," obliterated any remaining thoughts about trying to change my mind. Without an additional meeting, it was impossible for me to say I would pay the ransom.

The problems we had encountered in trying to contact the E.L.F. were fresh in my mind: We had hoped that Grant would fly the helicopter with Debbie back to Asmara, but the helicopter was on a remote mountaintop without a pilot. Haile, apparently, never had passed our letter to the E.L.F. The shumes had given us inaccurate information. The well-respected sheikhs of Afabet were spurned at gunpoint. Public pressure through radio and newspapers had fizzled; everyone seemed oblivious to what had happened. Tenneco's informant had given us false hope that Debbie would definitely be released the previous week. Our bargaining letters had failed. The final letter . . . *Nothing* was left.

Nothing—except God's promises, and I was not sure anymore exactly what they were. It seemed that His plan was not to bring Debbie back, but to use her death for some unknown purpose. I again puzzled over God's promised comfort. In the Bible the Psalmist had asked the exact question I was thinking: "Why are you in despair, oh my soul? Why are you disturbed within me?" With that question was an answer, and I searched in my Bible for it: "Hope in God, for I shall still praise Him for the help of my countenance."

Confusion and uncertainty, discouragement and dismay, still riddled me; but almost imperceptibly hope inched into my mind— hope in God's power. With hope came a new strength—strength to overpower despair. I struggled all day, desperately wanting hope to fill me. As I went to supper my unbelief still fought with God's promise of peace.

At that moment another letter came.

Certainly I never expected another letter. But when Saleh burst in the gate and jumped out of the car, I knew something had happened. Running over to me, he threw his arms around me, kissing my cheeks and hugging me in the Ethiopian expression of joy.

"Slow down," I said. "What's going on?"

"Mrs. Debbie—she's free!" he shouted in excitement. "I told

you . . . she will be released. Here!"

With that he handed me another letter, which he had folded tightly and held in his palm. Obviously, he had read it, but I was still skeptical of what he had said. How could it be?

Unfolding the letter, I read it without asking how he had received it.

Eritrean Liberation Front
    Executive Committee   Date 6/17/74 (4 P.M.)
To American Evangelical Mission

    The Executive Committee decided to release Mrs. Debbie in date 6/17/74 at 4 P.M. without any demand in a short time. Therefore, we want you to choose from these two points and give us your reply within two days; a). If you want to pick her up by yourself, b). If you do not want, we are going to bring her by ourselves to you. The committee also decided to cancel all the things which it was going on between him and you. We also decided to send our view with Mrs. Debbie. "Warning" If you want to come, please do not come to "Mario" or "Sheib" because the people there are not in the side of the E.L.F. Therefore, we do not believe them. Try to keep our instruction because of our security reasons. We are going to tell you where to come when you do agree.

Executive Committee

I stood numb. Perhaps I was dreaming. Was it all real? Where every possibility of sending a letter had dissipated—suddenly a letter had come. Where impossibly high demands had been made —suddenly there were none. Where Debbie's life had been threatened and all but snuffed out—suddenly there was the choice either of getting her myself or allowing her captors to bring her to me. Incredible . . . *impossible* . . .

"Where did you get this?" I asked Saleh, shaking my head in amazement.

"Today I returned to my house," he explained. "Some of them came and told me to go with them. They took me outside Ghinda —not far; maybe an hour. We came to Adam, and he gave me this letter and told me what they decided. I was happy . . . so happy.

I hugged them and said, 'Thank you, thank you.' "

After receiving the letter, Saleh had immediately returned to Ghinda and from there drove straight to Asmara to give us the news. The E.L.F. had given him no reason for the sudden change of heart, nor had he asked. He was joyful and satisfied enough simply to know the outcome.

Our shouts of joy were heard by everyone in the compound, and they came on the run. I hesitated to relinquish the letter for fear the contents would vanish. But it was passed around for everyone to read and rejoice. I also called our mission apartment and then Bob Perry at the consulate. All who had shared in the agony would be sharing in the ecstasy of God's dealing. The impossible had been done.

Saleh would return to Ghinda the next morning to carry our letter saying that we would go for Debbie. We wrote the reply immediately after supper to insure his early start. If the E.L.F. brought Debbie out of the wilderness, she would either have to walk or bump along on the back of a donkey as Grant had done. We listed three options for the E.L.F. to tell us the best route to take. Further, we wanted to demonstrate that our mission would keep its promise to help fight cholera and we wrote that a medical team was ready if needed and asked for more information and a guide who knew the territory. The letter completed, we gave it to Saleh.

Lying in bed that night held none of the struggle that had plagued me the previous night. Even my toes tingled with excitement. I looked forward to having Debbie with me. I would see her and hold her soon—the next day? Thursday? Perhaps Saleh would return the next afternoon to tell us when and where we should go.

Saleh did come late in the afternoon on Wednesday, June 19, bringing a reply. He said we were not to go for Debbie; the E.L.F. would bring her to us. I was positive the change was for security reasons. But where would they bring her? Afabet? Ghinda? Almost anywhere was a possibility. They might even leave her along the road to wait for a bus. The Ghinda area seemed most likely, however. After all, Grant had been released in Ghinda, our messages had gone through Ghinda, and Ghinda certainly was easy to get in and out of in the secrecy of night. Even if the release were not actually in Ghinda, at least it would be a central location.

I decided to travel to Ghinda the next day. For the sake of secrecy and Debbie's own safety, I would somehow have to wait for her without anyone's knowing. Should my presence be discovered, army lookouts would be posted in expectation of Debbie's release. Such surveillance would make any E.L.F. unit reluctant to bring Debbie out.

Thursday afternoon I could not get started fast enough to suit me. The sooner I reached Ghinda, the sooner Debbie would get there, or so I thought. As Saleh and I snaked our way down the road toward Ghinda, memories returned of the Monday twenty-three days earlier when everything had begun. I looked at the same barren hills and knew that my help *had* come from the Lord who made those mountains. Twenty-three days earlier I had descended the escarpment with fear and despondency haunting me. I was returning with eagerness and joy, scarcely able to believe it was true.

When Saleh rounded the last bend before coming to Ghinda, I settled into my hiding place in the car. While I pressed my knees behind my ears and squashed flat on the floor, Saleh whizzed through Ghinda. He did not stop to chat with anyone. Minutes later we were at the Steltzer house on top of the next hill. Once safely inside the vacant compound, I scurried into the stuffy, shuttered house. I gasped for breath. The hot season had swept in the torrid air and heated the house to 110 degrees. It was there I waited for my hopes and prayers to be fulfilled.

The Friday morning sun chased away the night's opportunity for a secret release. There was but one alternative: to wait. Thursday's half-day wait had seemed like half a year. I occupied myself another whole day, sitting on the knife-edge of anticipation, longing for reunion, yet without any notion of when or how I would find Debbie. Friday afternoon passed as I watched the sun gradually drop behind the distant mountains. Daylight faded into dusk and dusk into darkness. I closed the shutters tight to prevent light from shining out the windows and revealing my presence.

Eleven o'clock . . . still no Debbie. I concluded that her release would not be until the next morning. For that reunion I wanted to be rested and strong, to look and feel my best. But sleep came hard. I had looked forward to spending the night with Debbie. I wanted to hold her close and feel her arms around me. I longed for her gentle warmth to enfold me, and in my mind I kissed her a thousand times over. I stretched out, lost in the bed and alone.

All I could do was think of her. What would she look like? A month without soap or water would certainly have some effect, but dirt would wash! More intriguing were the thoughts of how big she had grown. When she had been kidnapped she was four and a half months pregnant. During the last few weeks that I had been with her, the baby seemed to grow each day. Perhaps I would feel the small swelling on her abdomen when I held her. Was my child still healthy inside of her? Had Debbie felt the early movements of life? A month was like a lifetime when so many new changes burst forth. Soon I would be a father, holding the child whom she had carried during those days of overwhelming difficulty. We would be united again as man and wife, we would be together—tomorrow—together—

The early morning light of Saturday, June 22, brought me no present. I peered out the window to where the beams of sunlight glimmered off the distant plains in the direction of Massawa. The day would be sizzling and sticky. As the sun climbed in the sky my hope sank. Five nights had passed since the last E.L.F. contact. Perhaps the letter had been a hoax. Time lingered eternally.

The clicking hoofs that had split the night that Tuesday, June 18, finally stopped. I held my breath and dropped deeper into

A Tigre woman carries her child strapped to her back. The tightly braided
hair style is typical of the Muslim women in Eritrea.

my sleeping bag as a whispering voice knifed the dark still air.

Sayeed returned hurriedly to the hut and groped for his flashlight. I recognized Bekeet's voice outside. Someone else had come with him, a voice I did not know. A message was brought in to Sayeed. Silhouettes danced against the hut walls as Sayeed gripped the light nervously.

He read the Arabic letter out loud, and then, without looking up, tore open another letter. A brusque command brought Osman and others to his side. After Osman read the second letter in Tigrinya, a muffled dialogue followed.

At once Sayeed handed me a letter and the flashlight. With trembling hand, I held the flashlight and read:

Eritrean Liberation Front
  Executive Committee
To Dear Mrs. Debbie
  The Eritrean Liberation Front Revolutionary Council decide to release you without any demand. Therefore from the date we wrote this letter onwards you are no more E.L.F. prisoner. And you should have to be ready for leaving.

Remark

You can keep this letter with you as a witness.

Eritrean Liberation Front
Executive Committee

I read the letter again, and in disbelief, I read it a third time. Through my tears, I looked up to see Sayeed and Osman smiling.

"I'm to be released?" I choked out.

Sayeed only nodded, then with a wide, warm grin, he handed me two more letters. Letters from Karl . . .

It had been more than three weeks since I last saw him. Much as a starved famine victim would plunge greedily into a bowl of porridge put before him, I unfolded one of the letters hastily and seized each word.

166

Dearest Deb,

I am praying for you constantly, Love, and pray that very soon you will have His Word to read. This is having an unbelievable effect in the lives of many and God is really at work.

Remember Naomi's words to Ruth, "Sit still, my daughter, until thou know how the matter will fall."

It's hard but God is able.

All my love,
Karl

Karl was well! He was alive! I wept unabashedly as I opened the second letter.

Deb,

"Comfort ye, oh comfort ye." Isaiah 40.

How I long to be with you, Deb. I am praying God will be glorified. Jesus' words are very real, "I will never leave you nor forsake you."

Know that I love you.

Karl

"How is Keshie Karl?" Sayeed interrupted.

"Terrific!"

"Do you want to leave tonight?" he asked exuberantly.

"Hedgie . . . hedgie!" I said in Tigrinya, "Now!" I had waited twenty-three days . . . I could wait no longer.

Laughter sprang from the hut at the ridiculousness of setting out in the dark. But there was not one man there that did not understand my excitement.

I reread the letters ". . . from the date we wrote this letter onwards you are no more E.L.F. prisoner." I looked again; the letter from the E.L.F. leaders was not dated! Was the letter therefore invalid? My stomach tightened. I showed it to Osman and explained the inconsistency. Was I being tantalized and prepared for something much worse?

Osman dismissed the question. "We will leave tomorrow," he reassured me.

Slipping the letters under my pillow, I thought more about Karl's letters. My heart sang in praise to God. Would I see Karl soon? I concluded from his letter that he must have tried to send me a Bible, but why had God not allowed me to get it?

The answer was not mine to know. "Sit still, my daughter. . . ." The hardest part of the ordeal was not in eating from a tin can, or finding my home in a shelter of logs, or staring at the machine guns the men held. Instead, it was "sitting still," resting in the fact that God was *yet* in control.

The next morning we moved.

"Come, Mrs. Debbie, get on the mule."

I had already been out of bed half an hour. Darkness still hung over the tiny hut. The night had been a sleepless one, but I could not have been more awake or more anxious to travel.

The last box was strapped to the mule's saddle, the sleeping bag draped over the top. I mounted awkwardly, straddling the mule's back. We were off!

We retraced our steps to the small village. The treacherous winding path of the sloping mountain fell to the empty riverbed. We paused briefly at the base of the hill that housed my first mountain hideout and the huts of my first friends. The sleepy huts were barely visible in the softly-breaking dawn. I scanned the plateau for a glimpse of someone I could recognize. There on the hill a woman meandered among the cacti. As she saw us approach, she motioned for us to wait while she made her way to us. It was Fatna.

Reaching down from the mule, I caught her hand. Her touch brought back a memory of weeks ago, and a picture of the helicopter chopping slowly in the sky. Was it really possible that I, too, was about to leave everything behind?

I looked at Fatna with eagerness during those parting moments. I wanted to give her something as a reminder of our friendship. But

I had nothing. "God bless you, Fatna," was all I could say as the mule responded to the swish on its back, and we started off again.

We wound our way through the riverbed that led into an unknown wilderness. The mule, its gait steady and slow, seemed unaffected by my excitement. How many days would it take us to reach Ghinda? Or were we going to Ghinda? One hour by helicopter, but by mule . . . ?

Two hours passed quickly despite our slow pace. Finding a shelter beneath a tree, we stopped to rest. Just two hours in the saddle, but it seemed like twelve, judging from the stiffness I felt when I eased myself down. I was disappointed at having to stop, and before I knew what was happening, the mule's saddle was removed. Two hours away from the village of my captivity and ages away from Ghinda! I could not rest until I rested in Karl's arms.

The morning wore into the afternoon and the afternoon into early evening as the soldiers leisurely bought a goat from nearby shepherds and cooked a meal for us. Finally, we set out again. As herds of camels passed in the riverbed, Sayeed asked me if I would prefer a camel over the mule. The lanky, lumbering legs of the camel gave an impression that it would be a faster animal. Nothing could be slower than the mule I was on, and nothing could be fast enough to get me home. Besides, I was tantalized by the thought of an adventuresome ride. My mind was made up.

The bags were transferred and strapped to a borrowed camel. The saddle consisted of two wooden bars attached to inverted V-shaped sticks on either side of the hump front and back. Where the single hump protruded in the middle, my sleeping bag was placed on top to form my seat. With its stomach buried in the dust, the camel posed for me to board. The men instructed me first to stand on the camel's neck, then to swing my legs and body up around the hump. I learned quickly that no matter how I shifted my weight, I was never comfortable sandwiched between the camel's hump and the saddle's front crossbar. As I clutched the baggage, the camel lurched forward–backward–upward–backward–forward until it had raised itself first to its knees, then to its feet. I felt two stories off the ground when the parade started again.

Three hours passed. Darkness settled over the mountains. In the distance a large bonfire beckoned us. Upon reaching a camp, hundreds of bleating sheep and goats greeted us. We stopped and camped for the night.

The shrill yelp of hyenas and the plaintive cry of Muslim shepherds at prayer were the last sounds I heard before falling asleep beneath a starry spectacle.

I awoke before any of the others, hastily straightened my hair, splashed water on my face, and smoothed my dress. Would I see Karl that day? My heart raced as I thought of reunion with him —of burying my face in his beard, of engulfing myself in his arms.

I waited restlessly for the others to rise and break camp. But Sayeed slept on. Why had he always to sleep in the daytime? It was time to be going!

Minutes drifted slowly into hours. Ten o'clock . . . Awake four hours, I thought, and not a step closer to Ghinda. The high sun baked my back. The excuse would be the same as yesterday: "It is too hot to move."

I was wrong. The excuse was that Bekeet was sick.

And I was sick with impatience. Why would God allow me to be so encouraged with a letter of release and then so discouraged by lack of progress? Had not twenty-four days been a long-enough wait?

I tried to work on my embroidery and then to write poetry. Nothing helped. I only bit my fingernails as I strutted back and forth like a caged animal.

"Sit still, my daughter. . . ." Even now, Lord?

Late in the afternoon I climbed on top of the camel for the first time that day. I was exuberant to be moving at last. The world looked beautiful and alive with activity. Baboons squealed from jagged clifftops; graceful silhouettes of large birds like pelicans swept overhead; rocks with purple and blue hews spilled into massive fortresslike formations in the riverbed.

The sun was setting when we stopped four hours later to make camp for the night. My tongue felt thick and dry, my lips cracked and parched. Twenty minutes seemed like twenty hours as I "made" water, dropping the purification tablet into a panful. How could I keep a water supply on the camel for the next day? I searched through my food box and found the catsup bottle with screw cap. After plastering everyone's supper with catsup, I rinsed out the bottle and had my canteen for the trip.

I was told we would be leaving before daylight. Everything had to be packed and ready to strap onto the camel. I planned to put on a fresh dress for the next day, one I had not yet worn. There was not much I could do about the greasy hair molded against my head or my flaked, dry skin, but perhaps a clean dress would spruce up my appearance. I thought excitedly of how I would prepare to meet Karl . . .

Streaks of light bounced from the mountain peaks to the hovering valley as we left the riverbed early the next morning to begin a steady, upward climb. It was Friday, June 21. We could not be too far from the desert, I reasoned. It was impossible to navigate the terrain by camel, so the men ordered me off. I worked my way carefully up the steep path, supporting myself with the same walking stick that had steadied me outside of Ghinda many days before. My ankles twisted over loose stones; my sandal strap again ripped from the sole. Osman tied it together with string, while I prayed that it would hold: "Please, Lord, protect my sandals too. You've done it this long, and it has saved my life . . ."

At last we reached the crest of the mountain. Scurrying to reach the top, I stood confused at the scene before me: vast, unending mountains. Three days of trekking, and we had not yet reached the plains. I consoled myself with the fact that while the mountains still seemed to fill the earth, the air was much warmer and the sun more penetrating. We had to be descending.

I mounted the camel again and we continued our steady march, picking up the riverbed. Gradually it expanded, and the mountains became rolling hills. We stopped for a rest along the bank at noon. The area seemed to be a kind of thoroughfare. Trains of camels meandered upstream. Cries of herdsmen filled the air. Families followed as they left the lowlands and moved to the highlands. Tea pots and wooden bowls banged against beds fastened to the camels' sides. The long curved hut poles seesawed with the camels' long strides. After a brief time our journey continued.

We rounded a bend in the river, where two men were lying on the beach, their camels strolling unattended nearby. A third man was filling a goatskin at a water hole. Sayeed went over to them. Returning, he asked me if I would give them medicine for cholera. The two men were dying. All I had were vitamins, I explained, and they would not help. There was nothing we could do. I had heard that hundreds were dead in a cholera outbreak. I looked at the men from a distance and knew they would be dead before nightfall. If only I had intravenous fluids, I thought, their lives could be saved.

"They must boil their water, Sayeed, or hundreds more will die." But even as I said it, I thought of the water hole from which Bekeet had filled our goatskin earlier in the day. Feces had floated on top. It turned my stomach to know that the goatskin was my only source of water.

The riverbed finally dissipated into the flat open plains. Following the escarpment, we bore right. Daylight was fading but not the heat, and my whole body dripped with perspiration. Looking ahead, I strained to recognize anything resembling a camp. I had been told we would meet Adam. But after three days' journey, I determined it was a hoax, an attempt to get something more from me or our mission. The release letter had not been dated . . .

We settled for the night near several Tigre huts erected in the middle of nowhere. A cot was brought for me from one of the huts. Although the sun had gone down, the air never cooled and in the fierce heat I struggled to sleep. The lightweight dress I wore felt like insulated underwear. The stuffy air clogged my nose and mouth. Mosquitoes swarmed about my head; their buzzing disturbed me more than the yelping hyenas in the distance.

Much to my displeasure, my camel bedded next to me. Acrid odors from its sweaty bulk nauseated me. As it rolled in the dust, thick clouds mushroomed over my head. At last I fell asleep only to be rudely awakened by a horrendous snort. Less than a foot away from my nose a hairy chin drooled saliva between a set of heavy yellow teeth. With a scream I darted off the cot and would not return until Bekeet had driven the camel away and diverted its interest to nearby thornbushes.

Early Saturday morning we continued our journey. Our path changed direction, and we finally headed into the desert. Nothing but scanty thornbushes and parched dusty ground lay before us. I braced myself for the merciless onslaught of the sun, but to my amazement a peculiar haze shielded its rays.

The camel plodded on. My eyes were peeled to the horizon, searching for a settlement, a road. A fleeting figure seemed to race along the edge where the desert met the sky. I squinted to take a closer look—was it just a mirage?

"There's your car, Mrs. Debbie!" Osman yelled enthusiastically.

I raised myself higher on the camel. "A car? What car?"

"The car to take you to Ghinda!"

Gradually I recognized the dim outline of a Land Rover. Other figures, with rifles jutting upwards, skirted across the horizon. More E.L.F.!

Soon I distinguished a small gathering of huts; then as we approached I saw Yakob's face.

"*Saalam,*" he greeted me as we passed. The memory of my first encounter with him flashed through my mind . . . his figure erect on the brow of the hill . . . my exhausted body prostrate before him.

"*Saalam,*" I returned his greeting as I was directed off the camel.

Adam appeared. For the first time since that fateful Monday morning I saw his stern face soften. With Yakob translating, Adam asked me,

"How are you? We hope you have not suffered too much. You

will go now, in this car, but first we have two gifts for you. The first is this coffee jug and cup. It has been made from mud by the Tigre people. The second is this live lamb." He smiled as he handed me the gifts.

The engine started up. I quickly gathered my few mementos: the embroidery veil, the striped material, a sliver of left-over chocolate, the first-aid kit and my soiled clothes. Then moving from soldier to soldier, I thanked them all, reiterating my promise to send Bibles. Bleating with annoyance, the lamb was shoved into the back of the Land Rover. I shook Yakob's hand gratefully before entering myself.

"Mrs. Debbie," Yakob began as he looked at the lamb, "you know Jesus Christ was the perfect Lamb of God."

As the Land Rover sped away in a cloud of dust, I dwelt on Yakob's parting words. He seemed so different. Yet as I thought, I realized that perhaps the greatest change was in me. I had been taken from a life often too busy to allow me to stop and "sit still" and see that God was God. But I had seen at last. God had taught me to sit . . . to know truly of His ultimate and intimate control and care . . . and He was granting me the privilege of moving . . . back to Karl.

Hours later a thirst-plagued party drove into a large compound in Massawa, the seaport town. I blinked in amazement at the rows of mud-walled houses, tall telephone poles decking the streets, and a pearly white minaret relieving the monotony of the low, flat-roofed houses. Beyond, I could see no mountains, no cactus, no men with rifles.

The driver of the Land Rover, who had introduced himself as a sheikh, took me to his home above a mosque. Mounting the steps to the second-floor living quarters, I was greeted in English by a tender-faced woman whose flowing Muslim robes fell softly over her hips and ankles.

"Come in," she said. "You must be exhausted. Oh, I'm so glad you're free! When I heard that this young pregnant nurse was taken

. . . oh . . . I felt so bad! Please sit down; I'll get you something to drink."

I cannot remember how many times my glass was refilled, but I drank till I was sure I would float. The sparkling cherry-flavored water was the best celebration toast that could have been offered.

"Here, you may use this telephone to call your husband," said the sheikh.

I thought the best place to call would be the mission apartment in Asmara. I was sure no one would be in Ghinda. Could I remember the six-digit number that I had seldom called before?

A series of clicks . . . then . . . "American Evangelical Mission," answered a voice.

In my excitement I failed to recognize it. "Who is this? . . . Sandra? . . . This is Debbie."

"Debbie? Oh, Debbie! Praise the Lord!" she blurted out ecstatically. "Debbie, call Ghinda, number twenty-five. Someone is waiting there for you."

"Oh . . . ! See you for supper!"

I cut the conversation short. Karl was waiting!

Saleh came to visit me at the house earlier than usual on Saturday morning. His troubled face told it all. He had been waiting at the hospital since five o'clock that morning, hoping for a contact or for some word on Debbie's movements. Silence.

As noon approached he left the house to find some fruit for lunch, and to inquire at the hospital about Debbie, just in case some news had finally come.

"If I hear anything, I will call you," he promised as the door swung shut.

I knew that everyone in our mission would be anxious. They would have heard nothing about Debbie, and since I had come to

Ghinda, nothing from me. Perhaps they would call the hospital, or perhaps they would call me so as not to alert the army guards of my presence.

Rrrrrrrinnggg. Fifteen minutes after Saleh left, the telephone pierced the dead-stillness of the house. I gasped; my muscles tensed. Excitedly, I sprang to the telephone and reached for the receiver—but then hesitated. In the three days I had been there I had never answered it whenever it rang, fearful of giving away my position. But perhaps it was Saleh! Had he heard about Debbie? Had she been released? I jerked the receiver nervously from its cradle.

"Hello?" I ventured cautiously.

"Karl?" came the reply—but the voice was not Saleh's. Over the poor connection it cracked with emotion familiar to me. It was not anyone in Asmara; it was—it was Debbie!

"Debbie?" I asked, afraid that I had not heard right. Her answer filled me. For a moment the world went black. My stomach churned in response to what I heard. The E.L.F. letter was true, God had delivered her, the release was real!

"Oh, love, where are you?" I could not move too quickly. Hearing her voice was not enough. It made me all the more eager to see her and to hold her. In a few sentences I had the directions. I would go to Massawa, an hour and a quarter away. At the near edge of town I would find her at the house of a Muslim sheikh. Impatient to join her, yet unwilling to say good-by for fear she would vanish, I finished emphatically, "I'll be there as soon as I can—and—I love you!"

The hastily made call put me in contact with the voice I had heard a thousand times over in my dreams. In disbelief I hung up the receiver. Karl would be in Massawa in a short time . . . just the time it would take him to drive there.

"Shall I draw water for a bath?" the sheikh's wife asked. Suddenly, I realized how absolutely repulsive my appearance must be. Although my dress had been clean the day before, it clung to me, wet with perspiration and gray with grime. My skin was streaked with dirt. My hair had not been combed that morning, since the one comb for the whole camp, Sayeed's, was lost en route. I thankfully accepted the opportunity to freshen up. Then donning a clean dress the sheikh's wife offered me from her wardrobe, I sat down to await Karl's arrival.

Twenty-six days of waiting . . . now the last sixty minutes . . . How endless! Finally the gravel in the driveway crackled beneath the wheels of an approaching car. Racing to the second-floor landing, I peered through the latticework. Karl came out of a blue station wagon, looked around curiously, then ascended the staircase to the living quarters. His rumpled hair, soaked shirt, and matted beard gave evidence of a hot, hurried trip from Ghinda. Feasting my eyes on him, I felt all my hungering for him satisfied. I ran to him as he reached the landing, and the world stopped as we folded into each other's embrace.

"Oh, love, you'll just never know . . ." His voice trailed off. A tear from his eye wet my cheek, expressing the hurt, the loneliness, that had been his.

"Oh, yes, Karl, I did know," I sobbed, clinging to him and gradually relaxing in his arms.

A smile shimmered across his face as he looked at the bulging bundle tucked behind my dress and added, "You've grown! How's the little one?"

"God has protected him, too. I feel him move!"

A short time later a small twin-engine plane, rented by our mission, flew us to Asmara. When I jumped from the step of the plane upon landing, my sandal strap broke for the last time.

Monday morning found us together at a small shop in downtown Asmara.

"How much for these?" Karl asked. He had begun to bargain with the shopkeeper for another pair of sandals.

EPILOGUE

We remained in Asmara for a week. During that time the "freedom lamb" provided the fare for a thanksgiving feast with all the hospital workers. On Sunday, June 30, we went for a day to worship in the small evangelical church in Ghinda. The next day we boarded a plane to leave behind the work, the people, and the world that had become our home—one to which we wanted to return. We left with what seemed like a new life.

Upon arriving at Kennedy International Airport, July 2, family and hundreds of friends crowded around us, singing, "Praise God, from whom all blessings flow." But as light bulbs popped and reporters pushed us to the wall while television cameras rolled over our toes, we realized our old world was no longer a familiar one.

Back in Eritrea the Ghinda hospital was reopened and all the missions resumed their work. A week after Debbie's release the first Tenneco man was freed, and in September, the remaining four walked out of captivity.

Also in September we both turned twenty-five—our lives continued together. But another life did not continue. Yakob had spoken of Jesus, the freedom fighter who was the perfect Lamb of God. Late that month we learned Yakob had been shot in battle —never attaining the freedom for which he fought.

Only Jesus gives life. October 16, eight-pound-fourteen-ounce Joshua, the hearty survivor of the nine months, was welcomed into our family circle. Joshua . . . "the Lord is salvation."

K.D.
D.D.